Canaan Possessed

Studies in Ephesians and Joshua

J S Blackburn

Scripture Truth Publications

CANAAN POSSESSED

Studies in Ephesians first published in *Scripture Truth* Volume 41, 1964.

The Land of Promise first published in *Scripture Truth* Volume 45, 1976.

Bible Study: The Book of Joshua first published in *Scripture Truth* Volume 47, 1980 – Volume 50, 1989.

Bible Study: The Book of Joshua privately printed as *Bible Studies: The Book of Joshua Chapters 1 to 12*, Keswick: A & C Bruce

Copyright © J S Blackburn/Scripture Truth Publications 1964, 1976, 1980-81, 1983-84, 1986-89

The Sound of the Silver Trumpets first published in *Scripture Truth* Volume 47, 1980.

Copyright © T Tyson/Scripture Truth Publications 1980

Transferred to Digital Printing 2020
This edition first published 2020
ISBN: 978-0-9511515-4-9 (paperback)
Copyright © 2020 Scripture Truth Publications

A publication of Scripture Truth

Scripture quotations, unless otherwise indicated, are taken from The Authorized (King James) Version. Rights in the Authorized Version are vested in the Crown. Reproduced by permission of the Crown's patentee, Cambridge University Press.

Scripture quotations marked (N.Tr.) are taken from "The Holy Scriptures, a New Translation from the Original Languages" by J. N. Darby (G Morrish, 1890).

Scripture quotations marked (RV) are taken from "The Holy Bible containing the Old and New Testaments translated out of the original tongues : being the version set forth A.D. 1611 compared with the most ancient authorities and revised". Oxford: University Press, 1885.

Scripture quotation marked (NEB) is taken from the New English Bible, copyright © Cambridge University Press and Oxford University Press 1961, 1970. All rights reserved.

Cover photograph "Looking northward past an olive tree on Mount Nebo, Jordan" ©iStockphoto.com/Joel Carillet

Published by Scripture Truth Publications
31-33 Glover Street, Crewe, Cheshire, CW1 3LD

Scripture Truth is an imprint of Central Bible Hammond Trust, a charitable trust

We are grateful to David Hughes for his work in checking the text and Scripture references for *Bible Study: The Book of Joshua.*

Typesetting by John Rice

Foreword

Some time ago we had it in mind to reprint the last articles written by John Blackburn (1907-1996) on Joshua in *Scripture Truth*, the magazine he edited from 1962 to 1984. Their theme is the light thrown by the activities of Joshua, in possessing the land which God gave to Israel, on the present understanding and enjoyment of all that the believer is brought into as a result of the death of Christ — now risen and ascended. Some only look for this to become a reality when in the Father's home in eternity, but the author makes it plain from Scripture that appreciation of our inheritance begins now.

A little research into his previous writings showed that he had taken up this theme in ministry over many years, and it therefore seemed valuable to expand the volume to contain his other writings which address the issue: "What is the Christian's Canaan?". In order of writing they consist of a series of thematic studies in Ephesians from the 1960s (full of references to Joshua), an address at a young people's conference in the 1970s on the Land of Promise (linking Joshua and Ephesians) and his final exposition in the 1980s of the book of Joshua (interpreting Ephesians). In this final exposition he makes reference to an article by Tom Tyson (1920-2009) of Crewe, and this is included in an appendix for completeness.

In the exposition of Joshua, of which he was only able to cover the first twelve chapters, the subject matter is not dealt with uniformly: some chapters are expounded verse by verse, others by theme. The final chapters are prefaced by the brief introductions written by his successors as editors of *Scripture Truth*.

As a sceptical teenager, I was won over by the grace with which John Blackburn responded to my awkward questions, and I quickly came to appreciate the depth of his commitment to help believers understand the unique features of Christianity: high amongst which are the worship of the Father and the present enjoyment of all that the death of Christ has won. I trust that the reader will come to share his joy.

John Rice
April 2020

In this edition further Scripture references, inserted words and explanations of obsolete English words are enclosed in curly brackets {}.

Contents

Part 1:
STUDIES IN EPHESIANS

1. Introduction

Twelve men, one from each of the twelve tribes of Israel, had been sent by Moses to reconnoitre the Land. Forty days later they returned, two of them staggering under the load of an enormous bunch of grapes, brought back as an earnest of the produce of Canaan. Then there ensued the most astonishing scene. This great host of people had migrated from Egypt (with overpowering evidences of God's might on their side), for the clear purpose of entering into possession of the Land of Promise; but they now refused to proceed. Four men stood for going ahead; the rest clamoured to return. For the time being the majority prevailed against the four, and they all turned their backs on the land flowing with milk and honey and set their faces to the wilderness. The few saw that country as the land of true delight which was their possession by gift of God, and were all for courage and obedience. The many were blind to the delights of Canaan under divine gift and therefore were not urged forward by its appeal; but they *did* see the difficulties and thought it not worth while. So for many years (in the cases of the individuals concerned, for ever), they missed God's best, which was life in the land of promise, and chose instead death in the desert.

"Now these things happened to them for ensamples, and they were written for our learning", and in order to learn *our* lesson, we, as Christians, have to turn to the Ephesian Epistle, for there we learn what is God's best for us, and are warned of the danger of missing it.

Every Christian knows the story of our salvation from the point of view of our own experience. It all began with the awakening of a sense of need. There followed the confession of the need, and the acceptance of Christ by faith, and the realisation that the need was met in Him. This experience is epitomised in the words "repentance towards God and faith in the Lord Jesus Christ." Thereafter, like Israel in the desert, we have experienced God's daily care and guidance. All this is great and good, but can anyone really think that God is satisfied merely with meeting our need, or even that God's activity in blessing toward us began with the object of meeting our need? In the Father's home He has His own delights and concerns in which His own heart is satisfied and the object of this Epistle is to tell how God has acted, out from His own delight before the foundation of the world, to plan and create a world in perfect accord with His own good pleasure, then to allocate to us a place with Himself in that world. This is the bearing of the phrase "according to the good pleasure of His will" (1:5). From the opened heaven God spoke, "This is My Beloved Son, in whom is all My good pleasure."

It sometimes happens that a girl — perhaps engaged to be married — befriends a little boy, to the great pleasure of the little boy. From time to time she presents him with a model Deltic Locomotive, or of Stirling Moss in an Aston Martin. This pleases him beyond measure, and he thinks of her as the best of all friends. But after all, when evening comes she returns into her own world of delights from

9

which he is entirely excluded, and so it must be in the nature of things. What God has done is something quite different from this. He has not given us good gifts and then returned to His own world. The thought is staggering when once seized. It is that when God began the story, long before our need arose, and indeed before our existence, "before the foundation of the world", He reached out from His supreme delight in His Well-Beloved to create a world to be headed up and filled with the fulness of that wonderful Person, and to predestinate His elect to a place in that world as their everlasting home.

The thought that God has His own centre of delight and action is further illustrated from the Gospels. Christ came to reveal the Father, and quite early in the gospel story He began to speak to the disciples about the Father. The contrast between the first and last words recorded concerning this revelation are highly instructive. According to Matthew 6 our Father in heaven stoops down to be concerned with His children's needs in their homes. He knows that they say "What shall we eat?" and "Wherewith shall we be clothed?" He makes the concerns of their homes His concern, so that they do not need to be anxious about them. See the contrast in John 14 to 17. Their thoughts are taken away to the Father's house in heaven. There is a home which has its own interests and joys, and His prayer is that their hearts might be there, as indeed, spirit, soul and body they will in the end be there.

When the moment came for God to put into execution what He had purposed before the world's foundation, His elect were spiritually dead and distant from God. This is the subject of the second chapter, which tells how God "who is rich in mercy, for His great love wherewith He loved us", has dealt with this death and distance, through the death and resurrection of Christ. When we were dead

INTRODUCTION

He has given us life in that we have been quickened, raised and seated with Christ. For our distance He has given nearness to Himself in that we are "made nigh by the blood of Christ."

It is, however, in the third chapter unquestionably that we come to the heart of what the Spirit of God is bringing before us in this epistle; and few would question that it is in verses 17 to 19 of this third chapter that we reach, in the apostle's prayer, the heart of the matter: "that Christ may dwell in your hearts by faith; that ye, being rooted and grounded in love, may be able to comprehend with all saints what is the breadth, and length, and depth, and height; and to know the love of Christ, which passeth knowledge, that ye might be filled with all the fulness of God." Thus to know the love of Christ is the corn and the wine, the milk and honey, the wealth and plenty of the Christian's Canaan. It is the pure delight of a day which will know no evening shade.

Paul's ministry was to preach "the unsearchable riches of Christ", and this prayer was for the possession by the saints of the true riches. It has been said that the world is like a shop window. We are to imagine a certain day on which the most extraordinary purchases were being attempted in a large store. It all started with what they saw in the windows. Someone had been round crossing the prices. Here was a mink coat marked at £5. Here was a camera with every conceivable refinement offered at 10/-. There is a piece of tinsel decoration priced at £250, and a toy motor car at £800. Only in so far as people have an informed knowledge of the true values of things from a worldly point of view could they be preserved from making fools of themselves in a case like this. The world is like a shop window in which someone has reversed the prices. Things which have in themselves little or no power of lasting satisfaction are valued highly and sought diligently. No value is put upon the things which are the true wealth, the real riches. With one voice this as well as other epistles declares that the knowledge of Christ Jesus our Lord is the real treasure. "The exceeding riches of His grace:" "the unsearchable riches of Christ." And to the Colossians: "the knowledge of the glory of God in the face of Jesus Christ — we have this treasure in earthen vessels."

What can we do about this great matter? We can do as Paul did: we can *pray*: and the very words we need are here put into our mouths. We shall learn that just as Israel had to fight for the possession and enjoyment of Canaan, so we shall have to fight for our Canaan. The closing words of the epistle deal with the fight, and at the end of Paul's enumeration of the weapons of our warfare comes the weapon of "all-prayer", as Bunyan called it.

One of the Christian's first steps in light is to learn what God in Christ has done *for* us, and his first prayers will always include request for our daily bread and for all our ordinary needs. We soon learn also the need for prayer concerning what God can do *through* us and others. But how slow we are to learn that so much Bible prayer is about what God can do *in* us, and the prayer in Ephesians three is one of the greatest of these: "now unto Him who is able to do exceeding abundantly above all that we ask or think, according to the power that worketh *in* us." Let us purpose now to pray often this prayer for a knowledge which passes knowledge, to know the love of Christ, to be filled with all the fulness of God, to possess God's best.

Since it is not the intention in these studies to go through the epistle chapter by chapter, a brief synopsis will provide a basis for tracing selected themes.

1:3. *Title.* God's activity in blessing toward us.

1:4 TO 3:2. *TEACHING.*

1:4 to 14. *God's acts* according to His Purpose.

1:15 to 2:22. *The Church.* The organism in which we are united to Christ.

1:15 to 23. Prayer for knowledge leading to the Church, Christ's body.

2:1 to 10. The consequences of union with Christ.

2:11 to 22. In the Church all saints are one with each other.

3:1 to 12. *The Mystery.* Finality in the unfolding of God's plan.

3:13 to 21. *The Fulness* of God prayed for.

4:1 TO 6:20. *CONDUCT.*

4:1 to 6. The Unity of the Spirit.

4:7 to 16. The Growth of the Body.

4:17 to 5:21. The Old and the New Man.

5:22 to 6:9. Relationships.

6:10 to 20. The Fight.

The third verse of the first chapter is a kind of inspired title for the epistle, indicating that the subject is God's activity in blessing toward us. This verse also specifies the realm in which our blessings are located — "heavenly places" — and the Person in whom they are bestowed — Christ. All the dominant themes of the epistle gather naturally under this head. This activity is according to *purpose.* In this purpose, the *Church* is the organism in which we are united to Christ. The *Mystery,* or Secret, signifies the distinct advance made when Christ was ascended and the Spirit given, so that the full plan, hitherto hid in God, could be revealed.

The intention in the pages which follow is to trace some of these threads through the epistle, with the prayer that the Spirit Himself may guide us into all the truth, and that we may find ourselves, as we tread these paths, in the living experience of dwelling in Canaan.

2. Heavenly Places

It was a gruesome experience for me, many years ago, to see a man fall from the top of an eighty foot building in course of erection. One can imagine three bodies of equal bulk falling through the air, a piece of rock, a dog, and a man. All three obey the laws governing material substances, including the Newtonian laws of motion. At this level man is the feeblest of the three and is likely to sustain the greatest damage. The dog and the man but not the stone, would be capable of emotional reaction. They would find this a terrifying experience, and could cry out with fear and shock. The man alone would be capable of spiritual response, could think of the consequences of such a fall, and even, in the brief seconds available, could think of meeting God. These thoughts illustrate the truths, first, that man is unique in the scale of creation, in that he has a footing in all three levels of being, body, soul and spirit, and second, that alone among earthly creatures he is capable of spiritual activity. In this particular he is like God and all other spirits. These thoughts in turn lead to the suggestion that at least an important part of the meaning of the phrase "heavenly places" must be the spiritual arena, the realm of spiritual activity, and where the spiritual conflict is waged.

"Blessed be the God and Father of our Lord Jesus Christ, who hath blessed us with all spiritual blessings in heavenly places in Christ." This is the first of five occurrences of the phrase "heavenly places" in this epistle, although the last is translated "high places" (1:3, 1:20, 2:6, 3:10, 6:12). It is possible that the same expression occurs in John 3:12, but apart from this possibility, the phrase is characteristic of Ephesians, and therefore careful study is warranted. An understanding of the phrase is necessary to understand the epistle.

That even unregenerate man is capable of spiritual activity is clear since conscience is active in him. Yet in the realm of spiritual things unregenerate man is dead in trespasses and sins and yet walks under the influence of the spirit that now works in the children of disobedience. The epistle is, however, explicit regarding what exists in heavenly places. Our blessings are there. Christ exalted is there. The saints are already seated there in Christ. Principalities and powers are there, and the rulers of the darkness of this world.

While, doubtless, bodily conditions react on spiritual things, and vice versa, the great emphasis in this letter as we shall see, is that by virtue of being spirit, man is accessible to spiritual influences, both good and evil, from God, from other saints, and from the devil and other evil spirits. Our blessings are spiritual and in the spiritual arena, or heavenly places. We are alive with life in the spirit, and above all can be open to the action of the Spirit of God, and also of the adversary the devil. Hence arises the conflict, and our actions are thought of in terms of grieving and hence hindering the work of the Spirit of God, and giving place to the devil and helping his baleful influences. The latter truth is particularly to be seen in the fourth chapter. From 4:17 to 5:21 the epistle considers the conduct of the saints from the point of view of general principles, as distinct from the particular relationships and hence duties dealt with in 5:22 to 6:9. The lives of the saints are to be different from the lives of other Gentiles because a different spirit animates them. The two kinds of life as seen in their actions and habits are called the old man and the new man. Intensely practical matters of conduct are dealt with in 4:25 to 5:5, and it is here we are taught that evil conduct gives place to the devil (verse 27) and grieves the Holy Spirit of God (verse 30). Action and habit are considered here in the light of which spiritual influence to which we are accessible they encourage or discourage, help or hinder. Especially is this concept elaborated in the sixth chapter where the writer deals with the spiritual conflict in the spiritual arena.

The Old Testament shadow of heavenly places is the land of Canaan. Long before Joshua, God had chosen a people for a land, Israel for Canaan, a land of corn and wine, a land of milk and honey. When the time came for God to put into execution His promises, the chosen people were slaves in Egypt under Pharaoh. God stepped in and rescued them and across the great barriers of the Red Sea and Jordan, brought them into the land of promise. They were by promise of God not only to be in the land, but possessors of it. In fact, they found hostile nations in possession, and they only possessed it in the measure in which they conquered it. When they acted in the strength of Jehovah they were invincible, and the only thing which rendered them liable to defeat was disobedient conduct, as at Ai. Nevertheless they never possessed it in more than a partial sense in the past. Yet Scripture is unanimous that they will, in the age to come, possess it, not in the measure of their faithfulness, but in the full measure of the promise of God, from the river to the ends of the earth.

All this is the clearest shadow cast beforehand of the Christian's Canaan, heavenly places. All begins with God, before all worlds: God, rich in mercy, for His great love wherewith He loved us: God, in the exceeding riches of His grace in His kindness toward us: God, according to the eternal purpose which He purposed in Christ Jesus our Lord. Out of the sovereign pleasure of His will He chose a people for a place, the saints in Christ for heavenly places. He predestinated them, not only to be there, but to be in Christ supreme, to possess all spiritual blessings, to know the love of Christ. When the moment came for these purposes to be put into execution, the people were dead in trespasses and sins (yet walking according to the spirit which works in the children of disobedience). In the exceeding greatness of His power toward us, He has given us life in Christ, supreme in heavenly places. Other spiritual beings are there: they see in the saints the manifold wisdom of God, yet they are hostile and a struggle ensues. An explicit contrast is probably intended in 6:12 — our struggle is not like Israel's, against human foes, but against spiritual powers, striving to make us fall. We have to reckon not only with our own feebleness, but also with strong enemies.

God's actions in the spiritual realm are to give spiritual blessings there, to choose, to predestinate, to accept in the Beloved, to seal with the Spirit, by whom we are united to Christ. Christ, ascended up on high, in this realm of action gives gifts unto men, and imparts, in the power of His might, strength to stand in the conflict. The prince of the power of the air takes occasion by the failures of the saints, by his wiles to hinder their enjoyment of their blessings in Christ.

The action of the saints in the spiritual realm centres on *prayer*, as in 1:15 to 19 and 3:14 to 21, and *conduct* which does not grieve the Spirit of God or give place to the devil. Above all, donning the whole armour of God, it is to withstand the wiles of the devil in the evil day.

Victory in chapter six is equated with standing. Our standing is in spiritual blessings in heavenly places in Christ, and these enemies aim to bring us down. The real victory will be achieved if, when the evil day is done, and we have been subjected to the wiles of the devil, we shall be found standing. There is a good deal in Scripture about another kind of fight described in the words, "the flesh lusteth against the Spirit, and the Spirit against the flesh: and these are contrary the one to the other." This kind of conflict is not what the Word of God calls "the good fight", and was never part of the intention of God for us. The good fight is to lay hold of eternal life, to retain our standing in the wonderful world of spiritual blessings.

When the wiles of the devil come to us, they do not appear as pink devils labelled "wiles of Satan". They come in forms dictated by a great wisdom, designed to deceive. Our struggle is against those great and mysterious spiritual beings, of whom we know so little, called in Scripture "principalities and powers". Their method is like that of the Philistines with Samson. He only saw Delilah, and probably never heard of or imagined the secret conference, "Entice him. Entice him, that we may bind him." Another hint as to their methods is in 6:16: the shield of faith is needed to quench "the fiery darts of the wicked one". At times, when all seems calm and bright, a thought, a word, a sight, suddenly sets us on fire. It may be the thought of distrust of God, or something that sets alight an evil temper. From whence come such thoughts? They are the fiery darts of the wicked one. The Romans used arrows and darts carrying fire when attacking a camp, with the intention of finding and igniting inflammable material within, and so distracting and confusing the defenders. We certainly have inflammable material within, and therefore we need the shield of faith.

In face of this fight and these foes, the watchword is, "Finally, my brethren, be strong in the Lord, and in the power of His might." How strange it is that any Christian is ever overcome, when we remember that the dominant fact about heavenly places is that Christ is supreme there. The exceeding greatness of the power of God has been shown in Christ's resurrection from the dead and in His exaltation; and it is explicitly in terms of His being *far above* these same principalities and powers, placed under His feet, that we learn of His present position in heavenly places. In face of this fact, how can any Christian be overcome? It can only be through neglect of the warnings and admonitions of a passage like this, and especially of this verse 10, "Be strong in the Lord." The real idea here is a passive one. "Be strengthened in the Lord." There can be no real difficulty in understanding this. Who has not had the experience of speaking to a human friend of the difficulties and problems, and coming away strengthened by his sympathy and advice? In how much more full and abundant measure is it true that when we come constantly to the Lord, there flows into us from Him, power superior to every power that can be against us in the spiritual arena. "She only touched the hem of His garment", says the gospel story, and immediately virtue flowed out of Him. If we came to Him more constantly, realising our weakness and need, and His love and the greatness of His power, then we would be strengthened in the Lord, and in the might of His strength.

The next direct exhortation regarding this fight is to put on the whole armour of God. The armour of God does not grow like feathers on a bird. If this were the figure intended, the Spirit of God would have used it. It has to be put on, and this indicates a purpose (still only in the strength of the Lord) to act in truth (not lying), righteousness, peace, faith, and to learn to use the offensive weapons of the assurance of salvation, the Word of God, and prayer.

We have considered in this chapter the meaning of the expression "heavenly places" as the spiritual arena. We have learned that it is the realm of spiritual things, spiritual blessing, spiritual action, and spiritual conflict. We can be active there because we, like God and His angels, the devil and all demons, we are capable of action, and accessible to influences in that realm. Perhaps the greatest impress we should take away is the privilege and importance of prayer, especially in terms of the prayers in this epistle, so that we may see the glorious Christ, live in His love, and be strong in His strength.

3. The Holy Spirit

"Christ ... in whom, on believing, ye were sealed with the Holy Spirit of the promise, which is the earnest of our inheritance until the redemption of the purchased possession" (Ephesians 1:13-14[1]). "The Holy Spirit of the promise": this name immediately takes us back to John 14 to 16. The Holy Spirit was promised to the disciples. Without Him they would indeed have been orphans.

On December 9th, 1934, in a deserted house in the town of Miaosheo in China, a baby, not yet three months old cried and slept alone through the night and on into the next day. On the hillside outside the town lay the bodies of her young American father and mother, cut down by the swords of a band of Communists. None dared to come near the house, for the Reds were still only three miles away. Could there have been a more complete embodiment of the word orphan than this helpless little life, so powerless in itself, surrounded by brutal enemies, and with no friend near? In the context of the new life within, the disciples would indeed have been orphans, except for the coming of the Comforter, the Holy Spirit

[1] H G C Moule, *The Epistle to the Ephesians: With Introduction and Notes*, Cambridge: University Press, 1891, pages 53-55

of the promise. What was the promise? The answer is relevant to Ephesians, for in 1:13 we are so distinctly referred back to it. "The Father ... shall give you another Comforter, that He may abide with you for ever" (John 14:16). "The Comforter, which is the Holy Ghost, shall teach you all things, and bring all things to your remembrance, whatsoever I have said unto you" (14:26). "He will guide you into all truth: ... and He will show you things to come. He shall glorify Me: for He shall receive of Mine, and shall show it unto you" (16:13-14). Where shall we find words to present the life, the peace, the blessing which are the potential of this unction from the Holy One? It lies behind all that follows about the gift and office of the Holy Spirit.

First, then, we need to know *when* we receive Him. We need to have assurance about this, for there is no part of the teaching of Scripture regarding the Holy Spirit on which there is greater diversity of view than on this question. When does a person receive Him? The definite answer is here in this verse in Ephesians we are now considering. In the Acts there is in fact a considerable variety as to the stage in the experience of individuals at which the Holy Spirit was given, and also as to the human instruments and their part in the gift. It is necessary to believe either that such varieties were intended to continue throughout the Church's history, or that some of them were special cases appropriate to the introductory phase of Christianity. We only need to hear the united voices of the epistles to understand that all but one *were* special cases, not to continue. There are two real questions. Is the Holy Spirit received at the moment of faith in Christ, or before, or after? Is the laying on of hands necessary? In Acts 8:17 at Samaria, the Holy Ghost was given through the laying on of hands, and likewise at

Ephesus in Acts 19:6. In all other recorded cases, the Spirit was given without laying on of hands. At the first preaching to the Gentiles the Spirit was given at the moment of belief, but in all other instances as a distinct event subsequent to belief. The usage of the epistles shows that the first preaching to the Gentiles provided the pattern intended to be permanent, and the rest were exceptional events for special reasons connected with the introduction of the new faith. In 1 Corinthians 12:13 "are we *all* baptised by one Spirit". Who is this "all"? All that in every place invoke the Name of the Lord Jesus Christ. In Galatians 3:2 the fact that the Galatians (who had fallen from grace, and were not running well) had received the Spirit by the hearing of faith, is made the ground of the argument as to how they were to be made perfect. But here in Ephesians 1:13, quoted in opening, is the most definite passage on the subject. They were sealed with the Holy Spirit "on believing".

The promise of John 14 contains the words, "that He (the Holy Spirit) may abide with you for ever". The irrevocable nature of this immense gift is emphasised here also in the reference to seal and earnest, and especially "until the redemption of the purchased possession". The Holy Spirit as *seal* gives final certainty to the covenant of salvation. The matter is finalised and settled and nothing can ever open again the question of salvation once a person is sealed with the Spirit. The thought of the Holy Spirit as *earnest* contains at least three elements. That He has been given is the certainty of our final entrance into the fulness of the life with God in heaven. The Holy Spirit is also the foretaste of that fruition: and this involves the fact that what is given with Him is the same in kind with what the saints will enjoy in heaven. What He gives (especially strength with might by His Spirit in the inner man, that

Christ may dwell in our hearts by faith) will, in quality and kind, never be surpassed in heaven. It will, thank God, be surpassed in the measure of our appreciation and response. The grapes of Eshcol were only in part a picture of the earnest. They were the very fruit of Canaan itself and therefore a true foretaste. But they did not involve the certainty, for the individual concerned, of entrance into the land. In this respect they fall short of being a true picture of the earnest.

In 2:22 we have the consequences for the saints collectively, of the gift of the Spirit. "In (the Lord) ye also are being built together for an habitation of God through the Spirit". The truth that God has ever desired to dwell amongst His people, and what was required before this could be true, is a thread which runs through Scripture. It was first known as an immediate consequence of redemption. "The LORD ... is become my salvation ... and I will prepare Him an habitation". "Thou shalt bring them in, and plant them in the mountain of Thine inheritance, in the place, O LORD, which Thou hast made for Thee to dwell in, in the Sanctuary, O Lord, which Thy hands have established" (Exodus 15:2 and 17). This was true in an outward and ceremonial sense. Since an accomplished redemption has been achieved by the blood of Christ, then there can be in an inward, spiritual, true and final sense, an habitation for God. God now dwells in His people as His house by the Holy Spirit. The central thought here is nearness to God, both for those who were distant and for those who were nigh only in the old outward sense, for we have access through Christ by one Spirit to the Father.

In these verses we have the church as the temple in verse 21 and as the habitation or dwelling-place in verse 22, and it is with the latter that the activity of the Holy Spirit is especially connected. In the Psalms the meaning of these two figures in the experience of God's people becomes clear. The temple is connected in the thoughts and experience of the saints with that distinctness and separateness of God in His holiness, in which He is the object of worship. The house is connected, on the other hand, with His people's experience of joy in nearness to Him. "I went ... to the house of God with the voice of joy and praise, with a multitude that kept holy day" (Psalm 42:4). "LORD, I have loved the habitation of Thy house, and the place where Thine honour dwelleth" (Psalm 26:8). "How excellent is Thy lovingkindness, O God! Therefore the children of men put their trust under the shadow of Thy wings. They shall be abundantly satisfied with the fatness of Thy house, and Thou shalt make them drink of the river of Thy pleasures" (Psalm 36:7-8).

Still considering the positive gain of what the Holy Spirit has established, we come to Ephesians 3:5. The new things, hitherto secret and hidden from the sons of men "are now revealed unto His holy apostles and prophets by the Spirit." These are the things which eye hath not seen, nor ear heard; they have not entered into the hearts of men, but God hath prepared them for those that love Him. The same Spirit who has sealed each believer, and by whom God dwells in the church, thus makes available in this place and to these people the knowledge of the depths of God.

This superabounding wealth of activity by the Spirit of God fills out the concept that the saints are accessible to spiritual influences in heavenly places, and it is manifestly of the greatest consequence that we should also learn how our actions can affect our reception of such spiritual activity on the part of God by His Spirit.

Before leaving the doctrinal part of the epistle behind, however, we find another element in the positive result of the Spirit's work, and this is the unity of the Spirit in 4:3. This idea really arises from chapter 2, the intervening chapter being parenthetical, though supremely important. Note again the reiteration of the fact of unity in chapter 2. Jew and Gentile believers have been made *one* (verse 14), reconciling both unto God in *one* body (verse 16): and both have access by *one* Spirit to the Father. The first call by which the saints are to make effective their response to God's blessing is to remain faithful to this unity. We are not called to make a unity. God has done this, and we are called to translate into practice the unity which God has formed by His Spirit. No modern cleavage threatens the maintenance of this unity so deeply as that between Jew and Gentile. Everything in race, history, aspirations, diet, worship and habits tended to separate: but to maintain it, the grace of our Lord Jesus Christ, the love of God and the fellowship of the Holy Ghost.

It might have been expected that the call would be to keep the unity of the body: but it is evident from the next few verses that the unity of the Spirit contains other elements than the unity of the body: there is the unity of the faith and the unity of the children of God. The "unity of the Spirit" also emphasises the inwardness of this oneness in essence, and hence that action in the moral rather than in the organisational realm is required to keep it. Lowliness and meekness, longsuffering and forbearance on the part of individuals can and do meet God's desire here, rather than the efforts of religious politicians to recreate an external and organisational unity.

The evidences of the fact of the presence and activity of God by His Spirit in the church appear in the Acts. Acts 5:3 shows the fact of the presence of God by the Spirit:

"But Peter said, Ananias, why hath Satan filled thine heart to lie *to the Holy Ghost*?" Acts 13:2 illustrates the activity of the Holy Spirit: "The Holy Spirit said, Separate Me Barnabas and Saul for the work whereunto I have called them."

The references to the Holy Spirit in the hortatory part of Ephesians very strikingly underline that the central requirement from the believer is behaviour which does not hinder the Spirit in His mighty works in the saints, but rather forwards them and co-operates with Him. There are four:

- Grieve not the Spirit (4:30).

- Be filled with the Spirit (5:18).

- Take the sword of the Spirit (6:17).

- Pray in the Spirit (6:18).

I think I can see a connection between the first of these and the Lord Jesus being grieved in the Gospel. "And He did not many mighty works there because of their unbelief" (Matthew 13:58). In another place He was grieved because of the hardness of their hearts. The mighty works of that Mighty One were diminished ("not many") by His being grieved. If no less a miracle than this has taken place, that the Holy Spirit of God has taken up His dwelling in and amongst the saints, where are His mighty works? We humbly thank God that we *do* see something of His mighty works in the saints. Why not more? It is because our behaviour grieves Him. If we put away lying, let not the sun go down upon our wrath, the stealer steal no more, the Spirit could take the things of Christ and show them to us. If kindness, tender-heartedness and forgiveness displaced bitterness, wrath, anger, clamour, and evil speaking, then more of His mighty works would be seen.

"Be filled with the Spirit" is not, like Romans 12:1, a crisis in the believer's history and experience, nor does it denote a moment when he "arrives". It is a constantly repeated or habitual thing. By the contrast with being drunk with wine, there seems to be a reference to our intake in spiritual things. If our intake is in the things of the Spirit, that is, the things of Christ, then behaviour will be dictated by the Spirit and not by wine. Read again how this also is illustrated in the Acts. It was when they forgot themselves and were full of enthusiasm for Christ that they became "filled with the Spirit" (Acts 4:31). Who could have conceived that in such circumstances their prayer should not have contained a single hint of concern for the safety of their own skins? They prayed for boldness in the cause of Christ, and for signs and wonders in His Name. These are the conditions when men and women, with the eye away from themselves, and filled with Christ, are filled with the Holy Spirit.

In what sense is the Word of God the sword of the Spirit? Akin to the fact that the Holy Spirit has been the Revealer, the Word of God is in a sense forged by the Spirit. The sword of the Spirit is Scripture as the Word of God. "Observe that the Lord Himself, in His temptation, the history of which should be compared carefully with this whole passage, used exclusively verbal citations, written "utterances", from Scripture as His sword. No suggestion could be more pregnant than this as to the abiding position of the written Word under the dispensation of the Spirit"[2]. "Taking" the sword of the Spirit involves

[2] H G C Moule, *The Epistle to the Ephesians: With Introduction and Notes*, Cambridge: University Press, 1891, page 158

knowing it, and the deliberate recognition that without it the enemy cannot be overcome.

"Prayer and supplication in the Spirit" seem to say that all true prayer is the outcome of the indwelling of the Holy Spirit. The Spirit poured out on Israel will be the Spirit of grace and supplication, and then only will their prayer be true prayer and reach the throne. Of ourselves we know not what we should pray for as we ought, but in and with our prayers the Spirit Himself makes intercession for the saints according to the will of God. It is because God has sent forth the Spirit of His Son into our hearts that we cry "Abba, Father".

4. The Saints' Union with Christ

The Church as the Body of Christ is a subject, not only of Ephesians, but also of Romans, 1 Corinthians and Colossians. In Romans 12 and 1 Corinthians 12 the purpose is to illustrate the saints' union with each other, and the members of the human body to portray the differing occupations of the saints. In these two epistles there is no mention of the head as such, and in particular, no statement that Christ is the Head. In Ephesians the purpose of the use of the figure of the human body is different. Although the oneness of the saints with each other, and the diverse functions of the members is emphasized, the prime purpose is to present the exaltation of Christ, and yet the vital union of the Church with Him. This truth of the union of the saints in the Church with Christ, stated, illustrated and worked out in its practical consequences, is a principal theme of the epistle.

The splendid position given to the raised and ascended Christ is the theme when the words occur, "His body, the fulness of Him that filleth all in all" (Ephesians 1:23). Are we about to be told that principalities and powers are the powerful enemies of the saints? Are there great names "of wisdom, love and power" borne by men and angels?

Christ is far above them all. With the Greeks the expression "all things" was a technical term for the universe, and there was perpetual speculation about its nature and destiny. The universe is under His feet! and He is its Head: and He fills it.

That Christ fills all things has been likened to the sun filling the solar system with its warmth and light. A better illustration preserves the idea of a Man and His world. One of the greatest names named in the world of the New Testament was that of Augustus. He is named in Luke 2:1: "And it came to pass in those days, that there went out a decree from Caesar Augustus, that all the world should be taxed." This great man was the architect of the Roman Empire, which gave the majesty of the Roman peace to the world in a system which endured for half a millennium. Some later emperors were, of course, evil men, but in his own day there was no corner of the inhabited earth which did not enjoy in good measure the fruits of the wisdom, mercy and power of Augustus. So, multiplied in the ratio of divine perfection to human limitation, when the glorious Christ fills the universe, there will be no corner of it where His wisdom, love and power in all their divine perfection, will not be a living reality: and this is the glorious Being with whom the saints are united in His body which is the Church.

The Church is His fulness. According to Lightfoot, this word means "the filled condition of a thing, whether a rent to be mended, an idea to be realized, a prophetic plan to be fulfilled"[3]. How can the idea be tolerated of

---

[3] H G C Moule, *The Epistle to the Ephesians: With Introduction and Notes*, Cambridge: University Press, 1891, page 64 summarising J B Lightfoot, *St Paul's Epistles to the Colossians and Philemon: A Revised Text with Introductions, Notes and Dissertations*, London: MacMillan and Co., 1875, pages 323-339

something needed to be the complement of so glorious a Being? At least a part of the answer must be to note that Christ is here a Man. The quotation from Psalm 8 confirms this: "all things under His feet." This brings us close to the thought that in the counsel of God it was not good that man should be alone, and Eve was taken from his body. In accepting manhood, Christ accepted this also, that He needs the Church to be His body, and later His bride.

As we contemplate these themes, let us recall that the words form the closing part of a prayer which asks that the saints may have divine illumination to receive them.

Some of the consequences of our union with Christ are then developed. In human affairs the fruits of victory are not enjoyed only by the persons who sustain the battle and gain the day. In a sense they gain the victory for the benefit of those who come after. Every good enjoyed by the individuals comprising a nation is the fruit of previous victories. A person alive in Britain's heyday stood on ground and enjoyed privileges (as well as responsibilities) determined by every event in the nation's long history, events through which the individuals in question did not live. By the fact of birth into the nation, all its previous victories — Ramillies, Trafalgar, or the Battle of Britain — are put to their account, in the sense that they are in a situation determined by these events. This is a faint picture of the way in which the fruits of Christ's victory are enjoyed by the saints in virtue of their union with Him by the Spirit. They receive the benefit of events which they themselves never experienced, and which involve victory over death and all evil, resurrection to a new life with God, and a settled place with Christ in heavenly places. These events, according to Ephesians, are Christ's awakening to a new life after death (quickening),

His resurrection, and His present session at the right hand of God. From the moment they believe, and by receiving the Spirit are made one with Him, they are on ground determined by His resurrection and ascension; they are quickened with Him, raised with Him, and seated with Him in heavenly places. In the original language, the verbs used here incorporate the preposition "with". God has co-quickened us, co-raised us, and co-seated us together with Christ. In addition to the "with" incorporated in the verbs, however, the Holy Spirit adds in verse 6 "in" Christ Jesus. The "with" is true because the "in" is true. The saints are seated *with* Christ because they are *in* Christ. These decisive events are behind us because of our union with Christ, and we are now alive in a world of which He is the centre, shedding on every part the beams of His love and perfection.

The advance of Ephesians over Romans and 1 Corinthians in respect of the truth of the Body of Christ has already been noted. A very instructive light is also cast on the relative doctrinal positions of Galatians, Romans, Colossians and Ephesians by the selection made in each epistle from the whole sequence of these sacred events: crucified, dead, buried, quickened, raised, seated, all with Christ. In Galatians, only the first occurs, crucified with Christ; and the truth of that epistle is in accordance with this, emphasizing our deliverance from this present evil world. In Romans, the first three occur, crucified, dead, buried with Christ. In Colossians, for the first time the resurrection side is reached, dead, buried, quickened, raised with Christ. In Ephesians, like the stones taken out of the bed of Jordan, there is only the resurrection side, and here only the final height is reached, quickened, raised, and seated with Christ, because in Christ. The question might arise, that the phrase does occur, "dead in trespasses and sins". This however, is a very different thing from being dead with Christ. To be dead in trespasses and sins is the disease. To have died with Christ is the cure, and this truth we have in Romans and Colossians, but not in Ephesians.

It is striking that, since the truth of Ephesians, "seated in heavenly places in Christ", was true all the time, the apostle withheld it in the earlier epistles. It would appear that either the revelation or the distinct understanding of these profound truths came to him progressively, as the need and inspiration arose.

Continuing our consideration of the union of the saints with Christ in His body, two points of interest appear in chapter 3. One is that the body is involved in the Mystery (verse 6) and the other (verse 9) that part of Paul's ministry was to explain how the mystery is being worked out in practice, "the administration of the mystery" (N.Tr.), and this leads directly to the functioning of the body in 4:8-16. There is found a description of the means employed by the ascended Christ for the making good in their experience of the fruits of the union of the saints with Himself in His body. And the means employed is giving gifts.

He that descended is *the same* who ascended. All the wealth of the grace of His downstooping goes with Him and shines from the place to which He has ascended. As the spoils of His victory, He gives gifts unto men. In this case the gifts are not, as elsewhere, divinely given capabilities for teaching and other forms of service, but these gifts to the whole Church are the men who have received these capabilities, apostles, prophets, evangelists, pastors and teachers. The form of the words seems to suggest that the last two are one gift.

What follows can be thought of as supplying the answers to certain questions about the gifts. The first question would be: What is their purpose? "For the equipment of the saints for ministering work, for the edifying of the body of Christ".

Much has been said on the subject of the true aim and intent of the use in Scripture of the figure of the body. Many have thought that, just as the human body is the means whereby the head acts and expresses its will on the outside world, so the members of the body of Christ are the agency whereby He acts and effects His will externally to the body. That this would be a logical and just deduction from the use of the figure is not denied, nor that it is the privilege of Christians to give expression in their actions of the will of Christ; but Scripture itself *always* interprets its use of the figure, and *always* interprets it as having for its aim the growth, development, and building up of the body itself. There is not one explicit interpretation bringing in the action of the Head effecting His will outside the body.

The building up of the body is effected by the ministering work of the saints, and they are equipped for this by the functioning of the gifts, and these in turn are the outflow of the grace of Christ (verse 7) as the living power achieving such result. Nothing could so magnify for us the wonder of our union with Christ as this picture of the grace of Christ as a fathomless sea, flowing out, giving gifts, equipping the saints, and so building up His body.

A second question is: For how long will these gifts, this flow of grace, continue to be effective? "Until we all arrive at the unity of the faith and of the knowledge of the Son of God, at the full-grown man, at the measure of the stature of the fulness of the Christ" (verse 13). They will continue, that is, until the Church is completed in heaven, until the building up of the body has reached finality in the measure of the stature of the fulness of the Christ. No intermediate, present and partial perfection can possibly fill out the meaning of this verse. It refers to the final perfecting of the body. Four goals are specified, at which all the saints simultaneously arrive. First, in that glorious day, we shall arrive at the unity of the faith. We have read "there is one faith". If there is one faith, why do saints disagree? The answer is that now we know in part; we have not yet arrived at the unity of the faith. "Thy watchmen shall lift up the voice; with the voice together shall they sing: for they shall see eye to eye when the LORD shall bring again Zion" (Isaiah 52:8). Second, the unity at which all the saints arrive is also the unity of the knowledge of the Son of God. This knowledge is full knowledge, to be attained when we know as we are known. Thirdly, the knowledge of the Son of God is Christian perfection, and hence the third goal is a grown-up man. Fourthly, this is shown to mean, not a collection of full-grown men, but one full-grown man, in that it is the measure of the stature of the fulness of the Christ. There can be little doubt that here (as in 1 Corinthians 12: "So also is Christ"), so imbued is the epistle with the oneness of His body with Christ, the expression "the Christ" means Christ and the Church, one body. These then, are the final ends to be brought about by the grace Christ has given. Until then the effect of the gifts will not be withdrawn. We have them today, either in Scripture (apostles and prophets), or in living activity.

This verse is one of the great provisions for the continuance of the faith "till He come". The saints are to break bread and so show the Lord's death "till He come". The Lord disposes of the lives of His own "till He come"‘

(John 21:12). His servants occupy "till He come". And to these we have here added that the grace of Christ expressing itself in the gifts to the Church, will continue "till He come".

A third question is: What is the immediate effect of the gifts? "That we be henceforth no more children, ... but ... may grow up into Him in all things ... even Christ, from whom the whole body ... maketh increase of the body unto the edifying of itself in love" (verse 16).

In connection with the truth of the Church as the Bride of Christ in chapter 5 the idea of union with Christ reaches clear expression: "joined unto his wife, and they two shall be one." It is because the saints are "members of His body" that the Church is the bride of Christ. Eve was first flesh of Adam's flesh and bone of his bone, and afterwards his wife. Just as, when it is a question of His body, the grace of Christ begins all, so here the love of Christ, in its original proof and its present continuing activity, is the fount of blessing. "Christ also loved the Church, and gave Himself for it; that He might sanctify and cleanse it with the washing of water by the word, that He might present it to Himself a glorious Church, not having spot, or wrinkle, or any such thing; but that it should be holy and without blemish."

5. The Apostle's Prayers

"Ye sought for David in times past to be king over you", was Abner's message to the elders of Israel; "now then, do it." This is the point now reached in these studies in Ephesians. In each chapter reference has been made to the commanding position given to prayer and to the apostle's own prayers preserved in such detail. The purpose of concentrating now on these prayers themselves is not only to seek to understand them and their requests, but also to say, "Now then, do it."

The two prayers are given in 1:17-19 and 3:16-19, and it should be a help to us in making these our own prayers to note exactly what they ask for.

In 1:17, the prayer begins by asking of the God of our Lord Jesus Christ, the Originator of all that is truly glorious, that He will also impart the full knowledge of it. Every word and phrase of the opening section underline the fact that, although this kind of knowledge can be learned, we are dependent on God for this learning by His Spirit. "May give unto you the spirit of wisdom and revelation in the knowledge of Him" is closely parallel with Isaiah 11:2 about Messiah: "the spirit of the LORD shall rest upon Him, the spirit of wisdom and understanding, the spirit of counsel and might, the spirit of knowledge and of the fear of the LORD." God *has* given His Spirit, but this request is for the wisdom, revelation, and knowledge, which are some of His mighty works. We ought never to be afraid to pray for knowledge, the right kind of knowledge, coming to us from the right source.

A very special light is cast on this knowledge by what follows: "the eyes of your heart being enlightened." It is idle to make anatomical distinctions between head and heart and the approximate distance between them. All knowledge must in fact involve the brain, that is, in the popular phrase, be head knowledge. The bearing of "the eyes of your heart" can only be, following the insistence that it comes from God by revelation of His Spirit, that this knowledge is also in a special way bound up with the affections. In other words, the meaning is akin to the condemnation of knowledge in 1 Corinthians 8:2 and 13:2 as well as in 1 John 4:8. Knowledge separated from divine love in the heart, is knowing nothing as we "ought to know."

Definiteness in praying this prayer will be helped by noting exactly the three points to be seized by this kind of knowledge. They are knowledge of

- the hope of His calling

- the riches of the glory of His inheritance in the saints

- the exceeding greatness of His power to us-ward.

Is it possible to exaggerate the importance and effectiveness in practical life of the maturing and stabilising of knowledge (as implied by "full knowledge") on these three points? Let us attempt a paraphrase:

- the certainty of attainment of what God has called us to

- the wealth of the quality of our Canaan

- the power of God to effect this in the face of every obstacle, shown already in the resurrection of Christ.

In our prayers we can go straight on to 3:16-19 which asks for our heart's response to the knowledge given. It is, of course, not desirable, or indeed possible, to pretend to certainty on such a subject, but it is practically helpful to prayer to see the golden words "that Christ may dwell in your hearts by faith" as the single request of the prayer. What precedes is leading up to this, and what follows are the consequences, and can only be the consequences, of Christ dwelling in the heart.

To cast the mind back over the epistle and see the tremendous extent of splendour and wealth in Christ as there set forth, and then to grasp the fact that the prayer proposes no less amazing an experience than that this glorious Being should take up His abode in our hearts, is indeed sufficient to make this *the* request.

This dwelling in hearts by faith implies the enshrining of Christ in the love of His people. It is an intensely practical matter of conscious experience and in no sense positional only.

For this dwelling it is necessary that the inner man (shown to be of God in character in Romans 7:22, but without strength in itself) must be strengthened by God's Spirit. The two consequences of the dwelling are seizing the breadth and length and depth and height *and* knowing the love of Christ. In this latter, we have seen earlier the heart of the epistle.

It is not difficult to see that if Christ is the centre of God's universe, then those in whose hearts Christ is dwelling are placed at the centre because He is there. This seems to be the bearing of the four dimensions. Only from the centre can the outlook include all four, breadth, length, depth and height. And it is at the centre of all that they know the love of Christ which passes knowledge. The love of Christ, and the extent of His down-stooping and of His uprising, as well as the "all things" He now fills, provide dimensions for the thoughts of God. Like a flower unfolding, so the knowledge of the love of Christ opens up out of the indwelling of Christ, and finally these experiences are seen to be the filling into all the fulness of God.

Our experience of these great matters will be limited, and therefore even our requests will not reach up to the extent of the thoughts of God, *but*, God can do *above* what we ask or think. In addition to all the other motives in all the other epistles, the things asked for in this prayer become from 4:1 the "therefore" of lives lived worthy of the calling. "Now unto Him that is able to do exceeding abundantly above all that we ask or think, according to the power that worketh in us, unto Him be glory in the Church by Christ Jesus throughout all ages, world without end. Amen."

Part 2:
THE LAND OF PROMISE

The Land of Promise

READ JOSHUA 1:1-11; EPHESIANS 1:19-23; 3:16-19

This article contains the substance of the closing address at a conference considering the typical teaching of the journey of the Israelites from Egypt to Canaan.

INTRODUCTION

Let us begin by going back to a point in time which must have been near the beginning of the forty years' wandering in the desert by the Israelites. Twelve men had been sent out by Moses to reconnoitre the land of promise. Forty days later they returned, two of them staggering under the load of an enormous cluster of grapes. Then ensued the most astonishing scene. This great host had emigrated from Egypt, (with overpowering evidence of God's power on their side), for the clear purpose of taking possession of Canaan. But now they refused to proceed. Four men stood for going ahead: the rest of the people clamoured to return. For the time being the majority prevailed, and they turned their backs on the land flowing with milk and honey and set their faces to the wilderness. A few saw that lovely land as the land of true delight which was their possession by gift of God and were all for courage and obedience. The many were blinded to the delights of Canaan under divine gift, and were not urged forward by its appeal: but they *did* see the difficulties and the giants, and thought it not worthwhile. And so for many years, (in the case of the individuals concerned, for ever), they missed the opportunity of life in the Land of Promise, and chose instead death in the desert. "Now all these things happened unto them for ensamples", and they are written for *our* warning. Let us see whether we can grasp the lesson, for the book of Joshua showed that Caleb and Joshua, Moses and Aaron, were right and the rest were wrong.

The shocking forfeiture involved in this turning back is underlined. If at any stage the question had been raised, "Why did the Lord rescue us from Egypt?", only one answer would have been final, true and adequate. He rescued them to bring them to dwell in the land flowing with plenty. All through, from the call of Abraham, Canaan as God's highest gift was in view as the goal. The story begins with Abram leaving Ur of the Chaldees at the call of God "to go into the land of Canaan. And into the land of Canaan they came. ... And the Lord appeared unto Abram, and said, Unto thy seed will I give *this land*." More than four hundred years later the time was ripe for the fulfilment of this promise, but the children of Israel, now become a great nation, were slaves in Egypt, and a rescue operation was necessary before the journey could begin. But the purpose of God's intervention to rescue them was clear and explicit from the first words: "I have surely seen the affliction of my people ... and I am come down to deliver them ... and to bring them out of that land into a good land and large, unto a land flowing with milk and honey".

During this conference we have been learning that in the Scriptures themselves this rescue from slavery and this journey through the desert are a God-ordained picture to teach us about the Christian's salvation. God has spoken to us of "Christ our Passover" (1 Corinthians 5:7); the passage of the sea (1 Corinthians 10:2); the manna (John 6:32); the serpent of brass (John 3:14); the springing well (John 4:14). "Now *all* these things happened unto them for ensamples" to warn us so that we do not make the same mistakes as Israel. And *the great* mistake was to choose death in the desert to life in the land of promise. We must now enquire, therefore, what in Christianity corresponds to Canaan, what, for the Christian, is God's goal in a land of plenty.

Indeed the Lord had said, "Let my people go to serve me", and we would be very right to emphasize the fact that we have been saved to serve. But the ultimate goal is something beyond that service; it is that we might possess *our* land of promise (Joshua 1:11). And I pray we may see that God intends this to be a *present* possession, as well as a hope for the future.

> "The hill of Zion yields a thousand sacred sweets
> Before we reach the heavenly fields,
> or walk the golden streets".[4]

THE CHRISTIAN'S CANAAN

What, then, is Canaan for the Christian? Our reading in Ephesians 3 does not mention Canaan! My first answer, it will be said, is an over-simplification. But I hope that a small measure of over-simplification is not inappropriate under the circumstances. Our reading was in Joshua and in Ephesians, and I will now add a verse, Ephesians 1:3. "Blessed be the God and Father of our Lord Jesus Christ, who hath blessed us with all spiritual blessings in heavenly places in Christ". Now here is our simplification:

[4] Isaac Watts (1674-1748)

1) Canaan, in the earthly history of Joshua, corresponds to "heavenly places" in the spiritual teaching of Ephesians.

2) The grapes of Eshcol and all the lovely fruits of Canaan correspond to the "spiritual blessings" of Ephesians.

3) The fighting to possess Canaan in Joshua corresponds to the Christians' holy war in Ephesians 6:10-18.

These three are special cases of the general truth that the earthly history of the book of Joshua corresponds to the spiritual teaching of the Epistle to the Ephesians.

Perhaps someone is moved to say that it has been understood that Canaan represents heaven and our entrance there at the coming of the Lord or perhaps by death. Do we not sing, "When to Canaan's long-loved dwelling Love divine thy foot shall bring"[5]? Is not Canaan the home we enter after this life is over? The answer is very simple. Israel possesses Canaan in three distinct ways. First, by gift of God long before there was any possession at all (Genesis 12:7). Second, Israel possessed Canaan in the measure in which they conquered it, and therefore incompletely (Joshua 13:1). Lastly, in the future Millennium Israel will possess the land of Canaan up to the full extent of God's promise to Abram (Genesis 15:18). Our present subject is the second of these possessions, that is Joshua's conquest. We are encouraging each other not to make the mistake of scorning God's gift, but rather to go on, to fight the good fight of faith, to lay hold of eternal life, to possess those spiritual blessings in heavenly places which demand our taking the whole

---

[5] J N Darby (1800-1882)

armour of God for the struggle against the wiles of the devil.

We owe to F. B. Meyer[6] sentences which are simple, true and concise answers to the question, What is the Christian's Canaan?

> "Heavenly places stands for that spiritual experience of oneness with the risen Saviour in His resurrection and exaltation which is the privilege of all saints."

> "The spiritual meaning of the story of Joshua tells of that satisfaction of rest, wealth and victory, which may be enjoyed by those who come to know the secret things which God has prepared for those that love Him, and which are revealed by His Spirit".

Let us take first "that experience of satisfaction". This is in exact conformity with Ephesians 3:18. To know the love of Christ is to be filled into all the fulness of God. The complete and unmixed satisfaction in the love of God in Christ which is set before us as our eternal dwelling-place in the Father's house in heaven, is open to us now, in this life, in the measure in which we set ourselves to possess it, even against the spiritual powers arrayed against us. Everyone who looks for satisfaction in earthly things will find it in measure. There are matters of heart's delight in earthly relationships which in the mercy of God are often experienced by us. But every person of mature experience knows that, though our hearts long for these delights, there is always the cloud of our sinful condition hanging over them. It is only in the love of Christ that there is that fulness of satisfaction which is the fulness of God. "Satisfied with favour, and full with the blessing of the

[6] F B Meyer, *Joshua and the Land of Promise*, London: Morgan & Scott, 1893

LORD" {Deuteronomy 33:23} is the blessing of Naphtali, and such a verse plays its part in pointing out the connection between Canaan and the experience prayed for in Ephesians 3. Let us pray for it also. Prayer is the last of the weapons which make up the whole armour of God available to us in *our* warfare.

Our quotations also included an experience of wealth, and this also is true to the references to riches in Ephesians (1:7, 18; 2:4, 7; 3:8, 16). One of these is in the prayer of 3:16-19; what God is asked to do for us in this inspired prayer is "according to the riches of His glory". What a person can do for us depends on his wealth in the things we need, and this in turn often depends on his rank. The phrase quoted means something like this: "according to the wealth of His illustrious rank". It is out of the limitless resources which belong to His unique majesty as God that flow the answers to such breathings as are here put into our mouths. One of the greatest things for us to learn, old and young, is where true wealth lies. I have quoted before the divine who said that the world is like a shop window where someone has been at work changing round the price labels. In such a situation, the only thing which will keep the passers-by from making fools of themselves is a true and just understanding of the real values of things. One of the greatest needs of the Christian is to learn where true value is to be found. In our subject we are learning that the true wealth lies in the Christian's Canaan. Teaching on this theme is not confined to Ephesians. To the Colossians Paul writes, "in whom are hid all the treasures of wisdom and knowledge" {2:3}; and to the Corinthians, "the knowledge of the glory of God in the face of Jesus Christ. But we have this treasure in earthen vessels" {2 Corinthians 4:6-7}.

We cannot leave this part of our subject without a reminder where the heart of the matter is found. It is surely in Ephesians 3:19: "To know the love of Christ, which passeth knowledge, that ye might be filled into all the fulness of God". Even in the prayer itself there is a build-up to this. Are you surprised that there is a build-up to such a tremendous thing? Here is the build-up:

"to be strengthened with might by His Spirit in the
  inner man;
that Christ may dwell in your hearts by faith;
that ye, being rooted and founded in love
may be able to comprehend with all saints ...
and to know the love of Christ, which passeth knowledge,
that ye might be filled into all the fulness of God."

At this point perhaps you feel like asking whether knowing the love of Christ belongs to our Canaan only. Surely the knowledge of the love of Christ belongs to our wilderness journey also? The answer is in the very remarkable types of the old corn of the land (Joshua 5:11-12) in contrast to the manna; the supply of manna, miraculous provision for the wilderness journey, ceased the day after they ate for the first time the corn which grew in Canaan. The manna represents the contemplation of Christ "come down from heaven" (John 6: 31-33), whereas "the corn of the land" represents the contemplation of Christ, not as sharing our earthly experiences, but as belonging to His own home and circle of interests in heaven. We find the latter in such passages as Proverbs 8:30, John 17, and Ephesians 5:25-27. The parable of the manna and the corn of the land is not nearly so difficult as it has sometimes been made to look.

THE JORDAN CROSSING

In our conference we have all the time kept central to our studies the light cast by the incidents of the journey, illuminated by New Testament teaching, on the manifold meaning of the death of Christ. It might well be said that the real heart of our studies has been the new light cast by each incident on that event of the greatest and deepest significance, the death of our Saviour at Calvary. The entrance to Canaan is to be no exception. Jordan is a well-known picture of death, and its crossing reveals to us that yet another of these aspects in that the death of Christ was necessary to our entrance into the place of spiritual blessings in heavenly places. But let us briefly review each section of our theme. In the Passover we learn that it is by the blood of Christ that we are protected from the judgment of God, because Christ bore our sins in His own body on the tree. The precious blood of Christ is God's answer to the guilt of our sins. But sin for us is also a slavery. In the Red Sea crossing and in Romans six we learn that in that Christ died, He died unto sin, and His death is our way of escape from the slavery of sin. But we also find by experience, bitter experience, that sin is also the fatal venom by which our nature is poisoned. The death of God's own Son, as typified by the Brazen Serpent, by which He took on Himself the condemnation due to this root-principle of sin, has liberated us from the control of that evil nature, to be able to walk in the Spirit given. The gift of the Spirit is pictured by the springing well of Numbers 21.

Out of the bed of the Jordan, at the time of their crossing, were taken twelve stones representing Israel. They were taken out of the bed of death, and set up on Canaan's shore. In Ephesians 1 and 2 we find what corresponds to this. The believer is considered as found in death — "dead in trespasses and sins" (2:1 and 5). That is not the same as being dead with Christ. The former is the worst possible form of our mortal disease of sin. The latter is the cure. Since in Ephesian truth, we are first found to be dead in sins, so we first find Christ in death (1:20). If we first hear of Christ raised from the dead, then it must be true that we first find Him in death. But Christ is raised, and seated in heavenly places at the right hand of God, and since we are one with Him by the Holy Ghost sent down from heaven, so we also are quickened, raised and seated with Him in heavenly places. We could not be there without His death and resurrection.

Perhaps you feel moved to say, this is too deep for me. Yes, and so it is for me. But part of my purpose is all the time gently to persuade you that God does not intend us to spend our lives paddling in the shallows. The best is yet to be, in this life if you are willing to go in for it, and certainly in the Father's house in heaven. But you must resist the constant pressure of almost everyone around to think that you have 'arrived'.

> Let no man think that sudden, in a minute
> All is accomplished, and the work is done:—
> Though with thine earliest dawn thou shouldst begin it
> Scarce were it ended in the setting sun.[7]

THE HOLY WAR

This brings us so naturally to our final thought from Joshua and Ephesians. They are both pictures which show the promised land as a series of battlefields. Israel, in the course of this story, fought many battles. But only one was the fight God intended them to fight. And that was the fight to possess Canaan. In this point appears most obviously the correspondence between the two books. In

[7] F W H Myers, *Saint Paul*, London and Cambridge: MacMillan and Co., 1867

Joshua we learn that Israel had to fight, and God told them to fight, to dispossess the inhabitants in order to possess themselves the land God had promised to them. In Ephesians 6, the particular point of view is that the saints are securely in possession of "all spiritual blessings in heavenly places in Christ", but the wiles of the devil, and wicked spirits also active in heavenly places, are ceaselessly attacking to bring them down. The aim of the holy war is to continue standing in experienced possession. Thanks be to God there is ample provision in the strength of the Lord and in the whole armour of God to enable us to withstand in the evil day and having done all, to stand. This fight is not a generalised struggle of right against wrong. Some enemies we are to flee. But these we are to fight, strong in the Lord. The prize is living in the experience of the love of Christ; being filled into all the fulness of God, the present fuller tasting of that joy we shall know in its perfection in the Father's house in heaven.

The two great themes which have occupied us at our conference have been the Cross and the Spirit. The Cross has dealt with every form of the chameleon-like appearance of sin; and the Spirit is the present power by which all this is made good to us. "Not I, but Christ" has been our watchword from the beginning, and on this note we close.

When the Portuguese explorers sailed up the east coast of Africa, they found evidence of a form of Christianity in a ruined church, with, still standing high over the fallen nave, a great bronze cross. Great bronze crosses have very little to do with a New Testament Christianity, but the sight stimulated words which have lived.

CANAAN POSSESSED

In the Cross of Christ I glory,
    Towering o'er the wrecks of time;
All the light of sacred story
    Gathers round its head sublime.[8]

[8] Sir John Bowring (1792-1872), *Hymns*, London, 1825

Part 3:
BIBLE STUDY:
THE BOOK OF JOSHUA
— CHAPTERS 1 TO 12

1. Introduction

1. Bible history has its *Peaks*, that is, periods when in the love, wisdom and power of God, and in accordance with His promise and purpose He introduces and establishes some new element in that Mount Zion to which we "are come". To refer to three examples, mention might be made, first, of the Conquest of Canaan in Joshua; secondly, of the establishment of the glorious Kingdom in David and Solomon, and lastly in the formation of the Church, when the Holy Spirit came down as the fruit of the victory of Christ and united believers on earth with Christ glorified in heaven. We shall try to bring out that the third is antitypical of the first; and that the Millennial Kingdom of our Lord Jesus Christ is antitypical of the second.

The word "peak" is illustrated by the upward march of events under the intervention of God, the attainment of a summit in the road so advancing, and, sad, sad to say, a decline when the working out of the blessing is in human hands. The ascent to the peak described in the book of Joshua may be considered as beginning with the *promises* to Abraham. Stages on the road are *redemption* by the blood of the Passover Lamb; the marking out of the

Israelites as a *people*, God's people; God's making His habitation, His *House*, among them; and, to complete the elements required, the possession by this People of the *Land* of the promise.

The fall away from the peak is marked in the following book of Judges by the introduction of the words: "and the children of Israel did evil in the sight of Jehovah, and served Baalim: and they forsook Jehovah, God of their fathers, which brought them out of the land of Egypt, and followed other gods, of the gods of the people that were round about them, and bowed themselves unto them, and provoked Jehovah to anger. And they forsook Jehovah, and served Baal and Ashtaroth. And the anger of Jehovah was hot against Israel, and he delivered them into the hands of spoilers ..." (Judges 2:11-14). This decline resulted in the complete ruin of what God had set up, ruin described, after the ark was captured by the Philistines and the priest Eli died on receiving the news, when Eli's daughter-in-law named her child "Ichabod, saying, The glory is departed from Israel" (1 Samuel 4:21).

There is the greatest encouragement from God, to be noted in its place, for faithful individuals in these times of falling away. They find a footing against the current, and find God with them in standing against it. But our purpose here is to feed our souls on the display of what is in God, as manifested in the peaks, that is, in the setting up of what is in His own heart, in His own power and grace. That power and grace is always available to those who "hold fast" what they possess, and to meditate deeply on these is strengthening to the soul, and glorifying to God.

2. **The Book of Joshua is permeated by the truth that God's people possess His written Word** (1:8; 8:31-34; 22:5; 23:6; 24:26). A very striking feature of the Pentateuch is the large sections during which there is no journeying. The camp is never struck, but great details are being communicated to and through Moses. Before the end of the books of Moses, all is written in a book, making complete the Law of Jehovah. From the Passover in Exodus 12 to chapter 19 verse 1 of the same book the people journeyed, reaching Sinai in the third month after leaving Egypt. There was no movement from Sinai until Numbers 10:11-13, representing a period of rather more than one year's stay. But during that year we have the ten commandments, the tabernacle, the priesthood and the offerings. This period includes the whole of the Book of Leviticus. After leaving Sinai Israel journeyed, until, after a period at Kadesh Barnea (12:16 to 20:22, where, among the legal enactments, we read of the Red Heifer) they reached a location of which the description is repeated several times, "the plains of Moab on this side Jordan by Jericho". The record of their first moving camp from this location is in Joshua 3:1. The record of their stay there includes the whole of the book of Deuteronomy, with all its content of communication from God, and very little narrative.

The written word named the "Book of the Law" was completed. "And Moses wrote the law, and delivered it to the priests" (Deuteronomy 31:9). Again ({Deuteronomy} 31:24) Moses "made an end of writing the words of this law in a book", and commanded the Levites to put the book in the ark.

There are references to a book (i.e. a writing) in Genesis 5:1, "this is the writing of the generation of", and so on: in Exodus 17:14, in Numbers 33:2 and in Deuteronomy

31:9-12. These Scripture facts agree closely with the existence from this time of the "Law of Moses" as the Jews understood it, and as the Lord Jesus authenticated it in Luke 24:44. The Book of Joshua is of great significance to us. It tells us of the first people who, like ourselves, were to be guided and controlled by the written Word of God. All blessing is in obedience to it — and all disaster in disobedience.

3. The Book of Joshua is above all the book of the Land of Canaan. The elements needed (apart from kingship), to complete the thoughts of God's heart of loving kindness and tender mercy towards His people, were only present when they possessed the Land of Canaan. To Abraham's seed were the promises made; the posterity of Jacob became God's people after the Passover deliverance; God's habitation was provided in the wilderness; but only in Joshua do we come to the Land. The Christian ought to allow to sweep over his or her spirit the earthly delights of the Land of Canaan, so that its spiritual counterpart in its turn may possess their heart.

The first expression of the delights of Canaan occurs in Exodus 3:8 and 17. "I will bring thee out of Egypt into a good land and a large, into a land flowing with milk and honey", and this famous phrase occurs frequently on into Jeremiah and Ezekiel. Notice the abundance conveyed in the word "flowing".

The Book of Deuteronomy provides the most exuberant description of Canaan in the immediate prospect of entering there. "For Jehovah thy God bringeth thee into a good land, a land of brooks of water, of fountains and depths that spring out of valleys and hills; a land of wheat, and barley, and vines, and fig trees, and pomegranates; a land of oil olive, and honey; a land where thou shalt eat bread without scarceness, thou shalt not lack anything in it; a land whose stones are iron, and out of whose hills thou mayst dig brass. When thou hast eaten and art full, then thou shalt bless Jehovah thy God for the good land which he hath given thee" (Deuteronomy 8:7-10).

The land of Canaan was not like Egypt. Egypt was a desert, irrigated by water from its river. No one saw the great catchment areas receiving the rain from heaven far in the interior of Africa and they praised their river for their prosperity. Canaan depended, and was seen to depend, on the rain from heaven directly. It depended on God. It was a land of hills and valleys as distinct from the sands of Egypt. This contrast between Egypt and Canaan, so full of significance, is quite explicit in Deuteronomy: "For the land, whither thou goest in to possess it, is not as the land of Egypt, from whence ye came out, where thou sowedst thy seed, and wateredst it with thy foot, as a garden of herbs: but the land, whither ye go to possess it, is a land of hills and valleys, and drinketh water of the rain of heaven: a land which Jehovah thy God careth for: the eyes of Jehovah thy God are always upon it, from the beginning of the year even unto the end of the year" (11:10-12).

We ought to be able to draw instruction from the meanings of names in the book of Joshua. Canaan seems to mean "low", and the word is clearly connected with humility under the hand of God. It perhaps draws attention to the feature of Canaan just mentioned, which must be reflected by the spirits of God's people in an attitude of dependence.

4. The New Testament counterpart, or the antitype of the land of Canaan is of immense importance, and perhaps it will be well to make brief mention of the

position of the types of Joshua as completing those of the earlier books.

The distinct series of types of Christ's death begins with the Passover (Exodus 12). It is clearly expounded as such in the New Testament; "even Christ our passover is sacrificed for us; therefore let us keep the feast, not with old leaven, neither with the leaven of malice and wickedness; but with the unleavened bread of sincerity and truth" (1 Corinthians 5:7-8). The passage of the Red Sea (Exodus 14) signifies baptism, and hence, "in that [Christ] died, he died unto sin once, but in that he liveth, he liveth unto God. Likewise reckon ye also yourselves dead indeed unto sin, but alive unto God through Jesus Christ our Lord" (1 Corinthians 10:2 and Romans 6:10-11). The brazen serpent, with its message of "life for a look", closely followed by the springing well (Numbers 21), are no less distinctly interpreted in John 3:15; 4:14; 7:38-39; and Romans 8:3-4. The passage of the river Jordan (Joshua 3) is less explicitly interpreted, but we shall deal with this in detail later. At the moment we must be content with referring to Ephesians 2:5-6.

This brief illustration of the continuity in typical teaching between the Pentateuch and Joshua brings us back to the question; what is the Christian's Canaan? The most frequently expressed thought is that it is our eternal home in heaven. So many hymns so express it. "When to Canaan's long-loved dwelling, Love divine our foot shall bring". And this thought is, of course, abundantly justified. Nevertheless it is equally clear that Israel possess their Canaan in three distinct ways. (What has been written before {in Part 2: The Land of Promise} must be repeated at this point.) Firstly, Israel possessed Canaan by title of God's promise to Abraham. "I will give unto thee, and to thy seed after thee, the land wherein thou art a stranger, all the land of Canaan, for an everlasting possession" (Genesis 17:8). From that moment, notwithstanding the Amorites in possession, Canaan belonged to Israel. Next, they possessed it under Joshua (which possession is our present theme), in the measure in which, in battle, the soles of their feet trod upon it (Joshua 1:3). It was not complete up to the limits of the promise to Abraham, but it was their possession which lasted until the Captivity. Finally, under the kingdom of their Messiah, Israel, repentant, cleansed and forgiven, and notwithstanding more than sixty-million Arabs, will possess that land up to the full limits of God's promise to Abraham, "from the river of Egypt unto the great river, the river Euphrates".

These three modes and times of possession correspond to three ways in which heavenly blessing can be said to belong to the Christian. Firstly, he possesses "all spiritual blessing in heavenly places in Christ" (Ephesians 1:3-5), and this is by God's sovereign election and predestination, before the foundation of the world. Secondly, he possesses his inheritance in heavenly places according to Ephesians 6:11-12: "Put on the whole armour of God, that ye may be able to *stand* against the wiles of the devil. For we wrestle not against flesh and blood, but against ... wicked spirits in heavenly places". The location is the same as in 1:3, heavenly places, but now possession and enjoyment are implied in the word "stand", verses 11 and 14. Then comes the final entrance into God's rest. In the exact context of the imperfection with which the people had attained rest under Joshua, "if Joshua had given them rest, then he would not afterward have spoken of another day. There remaineth therefore a rest to the people of God" (Hebrews 4:8-9).

INTRODUCTION

Thus we see the lesson of the Book of Joshua is so to fight
against the wiles of the devil that we make good our
foothold in the spiritual blessings in heavenly places
which centre on knowing "the love of Christ, which
passeth knowledge, that ye might he filled with all the
fullness of God" (Ephesians 3:19).

Here is justifiable simplification.

(i) Canaan, in the earthly history of Joshua, corresponds
     to "heavenly places" in the spiritual teaching of
     Ephesians.

(ii) The grapes of Eshcol, and all the lovely fruits of
     Canaan, correspond to the "spiritual blessings" of
     Ephesians.

(iii) The fighting to possess Canaan in Joshua
      corresponds to the Christians' holy war in Ephesians
      6:10-18.

I hope the reader grasps what treasures of spiritual truth,
understanding, enlightenment and pure delight must be
hidden in the seemingly barren lists of names delimiting
the divisions of the land between the tribes detailed in the
later chapters of Joshua. It has not proved an easy study in
times past. Let us pray that God will give us to hear the
word: "incline thine ear unto wisdom, and apply thine
heart to understanding ... If thou seekest her as silver, and
searchest for her as hid treasures; Then shalt thou
understand" (Proverbs 2:2, 4).

I would also not wish to pass without notice that, against
a strong current in contemporary evangelical thought,
great weight will be attached to the typical teaching of the
Book of Joshua.

5. The Divisions of the Book of Joshua

i. Israel's Entrance into Canaan: 1:1 to 5:15

ii. The Conquest of Canaan: 6:1 to 13:14

First Victories

The Conquest of the South

The Conquest of the North

Summaries of Conquests

INTRODUCTION

iii. The Division of Canaan: 13:8 to 22:34

At Gilgal

At Shiloh

Other Arrangements

iv. Joshua's Age and Death: 23:1 to 24:33

2. Jehovah's Charge to Joshua

READ JOSHUA 1

The first part of the charge, while being addressed personally and privately to Joshua, has its application in the plural and concerns "all this people" (verses 2-4). The second part is in the singular, and contains commands presenting the actions and qualities required in the Leader (verses 5-9). The rest of the chapter tells how Joshua communicated the reveille to the officers, and especially to the Reubenites, the Gadites and to the half tribe of Manasseh (verses 10-18).

VERSE 1

The Lion of Judah has been couched on the banks of Jordan (to quote Dr Edersheim), since the events of Numbers 22:1. Then it was that Israel "pitched in the plains of Moab on this side Jordan by Jericho", and the point from which the first moves were made under Joshua was the portion of the larger location lying nearest to the river. How long the Israelite camp has remained there we cannot say, and stirring events have taken place. The incident marking the end of the delay, and indeed marking the end of the Book of the Law, has now occurred – the death of Moses. Action of a new kind is now to take place, action to which almost every page of the Book of the Law has looked forward. This action must be under Joshua, the new Leader, and it is to him that the word of Jehovah immediately comes, so that from the beginning he may not move without a word from God.

VERSE 2

The simple facts dividing the wilderness journey from the conquest of Canaan were the death of Moses and the crossing of Jordan, and Jehovah's word made the reason and the action exquisitely clear. "Moses my servant is dead; now therefore arise, go over this Jordan, thou and all this people, unto the land which I do give unto them."

On the scale of merely human history, Moses must have claims to be the most illustrious man who ever lived; sole and effective leader of a mass migration of six hundred thousand men, with the women and children, for forty years; the only writer in the second millennium B.C. whose work generally and across the nations is printed, sold and read with avidity at the end of the second millennium A.D.; lawgiver whose code has influenced every code since his time. The divine estimate is, of course much more important: "there arose not a prophet since in Israel like unto Moses, whom the LORD knew face to face" {Deuteronomy 34:10}. The passing of such a man, and the entrance of Joshua into an enterprise so entirely unknown, as a sole leader, must be moment for pause and earnest consideration. The fact is, and must be understood, that in spite of undimmed eye and unabated natural force, Moses cannot bring Israel into Canaan. The importance of this fact for the Christian, is to be seen in the type. The law has no place in giving us entrance into the spiritual blessings in heavenly places. The purpose of God above all dispensation, and the resurrection of Jesus from the dead, and his taking His seat on high, are the ground on which such blessing can be ours. The law is holy and just and good, but could never give life. Only the risen and ascended Lord can lead us in, and of Him Joshua is the type.

Care is needed to distinguish what was true for Israel and Canaan from what belongs to the Christian and their spiritual blessings. Israel did enter in under the covenant of law, and hence they could not fully possess. The book of the Law which was to be Joshua's ceaseless study, represents for us "the word of Christ dwelling in us richly" (Colossians 3:16).

The second sentence of the verse contains the command, and every phrase is a trumpet call. The first of Scripture's numerous commands to "arise" is God's direction to Abraham: "Arise, walk through the land in the length of it and in the breadth of it; for I will give it unto thee" (Genesis 13:17). Perhaps in the setting, Abraham's walk was determined in its extent by verse 14 of the same chapter, rather than 15:18. In its place the patient and detailed survey involved in Abraham's placing the soles of his feet across the length and breadth of the land is perhaps another and necessary call to action for the Christian, but in our chapter it is possession and not survey which comes before us. *Arise* Joshua! Strike the camp; marshal the host; order the march; there is much to do.

The immediate action was not complicated. They were to cross the mystic barrier, to take up a position *in the land*. The action was decisive, and from that moment, they were committed. Many, many Christians are satisfied with the life in which they experience the guidance of God, the divine provision, and indeed the presence of God with them in their earthly circumstances, and in the service appropriate to such life. All these things constitute the life typified by the wilderness journey. Such experiences are good, very good. But it could not be more clear and compelling that this is not God's *purpose* for His people. The clarity of the difference is so vivid, so inescapable, as illuminated by these types, that it is small wonder that if we wish to be satisfied with the life of the wilderness, we will not wish to believe in typical teaching. To take up a position in Canaan is to experience the illumination by which we perceive as something open to be enjoyed by us, our union with Christ in heavenly places with all its tremendous consequences centred on Ephesians 5:25(b)-27 and 3:19. Such perceptions are the first step to possessing our entitlement. Such are the reasons for the precedence of the prayer of Ephesians chapter one over that of chapter three.

The demonstrative "this" is a gently compelling feature in this chapter. In verse 4 we find "this Lebanon"; in verse 8 "this book of the law"; and twice, verses 2 and 11, "this Jordan". It is difficult to escape the impression that the objects so marked out were visible before their eyes. Suffice for the moment to note this emphasis. The significance of the river in these types will come before us in Joshua chapter 3.

VERSES 3-5

These verses are a quotation of Deuteronomy 11:24-25(a), and put Joshua under the same promise and assurance as was Moses, regarding the limits of their conquest of Canaan. Exactly what land is promised to Israel is a subject of importance from several points of view, and we must give thought to it.

First, let us notice the difference between the passages in Deuteronomy and Joshua. The first is "this" Lebanon. Although the words were spoken to Moses in approximately the same location, it is evident that to Joshua everything is more immediately before him both in time and space. I think we must understand that Joshua could see the Lebanon range. Next, the quotation is amplified by addition of the words "all the land of the Hittites". This perhaps stresses the meaning of the name "sons of terror", and contains an assurance to Joshua who long before refused to be dismayed by the giants reported by the spies. The opening words of verse 5, which in Deuteronomy are in the plural ("stand before *you*"), are in our chapter in the singular, and stand as the first of the personal assurances of Jehovah to Joshua as the new fighting leader.

The boundaries described in verse 4 identify the land which lay before Israel as the land promised to Abram (Genesis 15:18), and the promise is now confirmed. The "I do give" of verse 2 declares the present intention of Jehovah, to be fulfilled in this book of Scripture. The "I have given" of verse 3 refers to the promise already made to Moses. Thus we must understand the limits which now lie before us to be an amplification of Genesis 15. In these places the land is described in terms of the great natural barriers which enclose it. In Genesis 15 they are "from the River (Hebrew *nahar*) unto the great river, the River Euphrates". The word *nahar* identifies a great river aligned in size and importance with the Euphrates, that is, the Nile. (It cannot mean the Brook of Egypt [Joshua 15:4, Hebrew *nachal*] which means a valley torrent, so common in Palestine.) Three further barriers are now introduced: the "Wilderness", "this Lebanon", and the "great sea" – the Mediterranean. These five are all great natural barriers, and not lines of border villages as in other places.

The great stretch of Wilderness (desert) – Sinai, Jordan and Syria, all fringes of the immense Arabian Desert, stretching round the south and east of Canaan – is a prominent feature of the geography of the Near East. This feature determines the portion of the Euphrates intended. Is it the whole river from source to the Persian Gulf, or only a portion of this? It is that stretch of the great river which runs from its source in Armenia, across the north-eastern edge of Syria, until the desert interposes itself as the barrier nearest to Canaan.

The Lebanon ranges are manifestly a very striking natural barrier to the north of Canaan. The word Lebanon means "the white mountain". Several summits are in permanent snow. The familiar photographs of one of the long, snow-covered summits, show a face presented to the east, and it is the south ends of Lebanon, Anti-lebano and Hermon which form the natural frontier.

These five natural frontiers enclose Palestine and include the whole of the coastal strip, the habitable parts of Syria, Jordan and a fragment of Egypt. We shall see in this Book details in which the conquest described came short of these borders. Verse 4 gives assurance to Joshua that there would be nothing in the mind and intention of the God of Israel to cause Israel to fall short. The land in its totality, so promised and described, was never, even under David, included with stability in the land of Israel, but the promises remain, and what was impossible under the covenant of law will surely be accomplished under the covenant of promise. Likewise for the Christian, what cannot be apprehended in its fullness now, will surely be ours in its fullness according to the purpose of God and the love and the sacrifice of Christ.

VERSES 5-6

We now enter on the commands addressed to Joshua personally and in the singular. We can thus take them, like so many Psalms, directly to ourselves as principles of godliness above all dispensations, and unchanged throughout Scripture. Verse 5 contains an assurance without which Joshua dare not take a single step – the assurance of the personal presence of Jehovah at his side "all the days". See how this golden phrase is uttered by the Lord for all the circumstances of all His people. It applies to Jehovah's care for His people in the wilderness: "In all their affliction he was afflicted, and the angel of his presence saved them: in his love and in his pity he redeemed them, and he bare them, and carried them *all the days* of old" (Isaiah 63:9). It is here repeated personally to Joshua: "There shall not any man be able to stand before thee *all the days* of thy life, … I will be with thee". How often the familiar words of Psalm 23 have spoken to us: "Surely goodness and mercy shall follow me *all the days* of my life, and I will dwell in the house of the Lord for ever". How the days differ! There is the good and sunny day, and there is the woefully evil day. There are days of strife and days of peace, but all are under the last words of the Saviour in Matthew's Gospel, literally translated: "Lo, I am with you *all the days* unto the end of the world".

The last words of verse 5 are quoted in Hebrews 13:5 in a setting which assures us that the promises concerning godliness found in the Old Testament are directly available to the Christian. This Scripture appeals to me as a most precious example of the use of the "shield of faith" against the "fiery darts" of the Wicked One, and therefore appropriate to the fight for our Canaan. The injection into mind and heart of the thought that we are "on our own", that God has forgotten us is indeed a fiery dart. Such a dart finds inflammable material within us when faith is feeble, and passionate feelings of distrust of God may flare up. It is for all such flames of passion that the shield of faith is provided, faith which lays hold of a word of God and claims its truth against all appearances. How many times when the pressures were most fierce must Joshua have spoken to his heart: *Jehovah* hath said, "I will never leave thee, nor forsake thee," so that *I* may boldly say, (another word of Scripture – Psalm 118:6) "I *will not* fear what man shall do unto me".

This promise of the unfailing presence and nearness of the Lord forms the basis for the stirring charge to "be strong and of good courage" which follows in verse 6. Strength and courage were vital, not only for himself, but also as Leader, so as to inspire the hosts who were to follow him and receive from him their inheritance in the land. So it is for us. Once the heart and spirit of the believer are awakened to the wealth of "hid treasure" open to him through his union with the ascended Christ, then the power needed for the struggle immediately deals with this need.

Who and what are against us? We shall experience their existence and drive the moment we set ourselves to possess and stand in our spiritual heritage. "The principalities ... the powers ... and world-rulers of this darkness ... the spiritual hosts of wickedness in the heavenly places". In the arena of this struggle, whatever may be the opposition visible in fellow-men of flesh and blood, we must see past them to the mysterious but real powers revealed to us in this verse (Ephesians 6:12, RV) as also in 2:2 "the prince of the power of the air, the spirit that now worketh in the children of disobedience".

Who and what is to be our strength? Is it possible for us to be adequately empowered? Ephesians 6:10 is the counterpart of Joshua 1:6. "Be strong in the Lord, and in the power of his might". The occurrence several times of these three words in the same context in Ephesians is notable – (AV) strength, power, might. The engineering concepts and definitions of strength, work, power, energy, and the like, doubtless do not correspond to the range of words used in these Scriptures. But they do illustrate the many-sided completeness of the power resident in God and in His Christ. Read carefully the following passages in the Epistle to the Ephesians and note the frequency of these words: 1:19-20 (the doctrine); 3:16, 20 (the prayer); 6:10 (the warfare). Do they not demonstrate all the fullness that lies behind the provision for the warfare in heavenly places: "Be strong and of a good courage"?

VERSES 7-9

In these verses the words to be underlined are "only" (verse 7) and "then" (verse 8). The previous verses have emphasised the "I" of all Jehovah's doing: "I do give"; "I have given"; "I will be with thee"; "I will not forsake thee"; "I sware unto" your fathers. The "only" thus signifies, "Since I, Jehovah have charged myself with the burden of *all* that is needed to ensure prosperity and good success, *you* have only two things to consider, courage and obedience". And the "then" signifies, "Granted that you on your part grasp these two opportunities, *then* you are guaranteed that 'thou shalt make thy way prosperous, and *then* thou shalt have good success'".

Strategy, and tactics, ambushes, night marches, stratagems and surprise attacks are all to be found in the story. These directions are not to say that these means and many other marks of generalship are not required; but they do say that, with Jehovah himself by your side, it is all in the book.

Strength and courage have been the subjects of verse 6, but obedience is now insistently required. Here on this page of Scripture there stands before us the very first man, and the very first people who possessed the written word of God. The "strength and courage", the energy and the decisive action are required in the first place "to observe to do" according to that word. Here is the point at which the opposition of spiritual powers to your stand in Canaan begins. If you fail here, it is unlikely that later lessons will bear their fruit. In the special sense of our study of the Book of Joshua, to observe the action pressed with such energy and concentration is not only to enjoy an expository exercise, but to expose ourselves to stimulus to such action in the spiritual arena. "Turn not from it – it shall not depart out of thy mouth – meditate therein day and night". Joshua, and all who learn this lesson will be like the righteous man of Psalm 1 who meditates in the law of the Lord day and night, and likewise enjoys prosperity.

Meditation is a means of grace most greatly to be esteemed. Whatever may be the method adopted, meditation essentially is a means of prolonging the exposure of mind and affections to the beneficent action of the Word. It means, not being satisfied with the first exposure, when the Word is heard or read, but returning to the portion which has come before us, and so giving the Word itself time to produce the effect upon us for which it was "sent forth". Read verse 8 again. Do you not feel in your heart its grip and drive? What apart from God's Word could reach out like this across the centuries and the translations, and fit us men and women as the key fits the lock?

VERSES 10-18

The people are instructed to make preparations for the Jordan crossing, and this applies also to the two tribes and a half of which we read in Numbers 31. For the moment all appears to be in order with them, for the land they chose was within the land of promise. But it was chosen by themselves and not by God, and it is for this reason reminiscent of Lot and the choice he made. At best they seem to represent those who are satisfied with peripheral blessings, rather than that which is really Canaan.

3. Rahab's Faith

READ JOSHUA 2

We are introduced in this chapter to two individuals among the thousands of Canaanites, whose destruction had come so near (verses 1-7). One of these, Rahab, makes a very full confession of her knowledge and faith (verses 8-13), and makes a plea for shelter under the wings of the God of Israel (verses 12-13). The spies pledge Rahab's salvation from the impending destruction of the city, together with her father's household (verses 14-17), give her a token in the scarlet cord (verses 18-20) and, after three days' hiding, returned across the river to Joshua (verses 21-24).

In seeking to seize the lessons of this narrative, we return to the thought, just mentioned, that here is a view of the thoughts and actions of two individuals during "the last days of" Jericho. The king need not detain us long. Kingship is a most important concept in Scripture, and "king" is one of the words frequently recurring in this book of Scripture. The typical meaning of these petty kings of Canaan is not far to seek, and will come before us in studying later chapters.

The case of Rahab is different, in that she is singled out three times for mention in the New Testament. She is introduced in verse 1; they, "came into a harlot's house, named Rahab, and lodged there". She makes an immediate impression as a resourceful woman, ready for immediate decision and action. But she was an evil member of an accursed race, even if not a priestess of the Canaanite religion. Such is the person in Jericho to whom the God of Israel had reached out His hand, and granted her convictions which bring her into salvation. The narrative before us provides occasion for reflection on three themes:

1. "The wrath to come".

2. "By faith Rahab ... perished not".

3. "Thou shalt utterly destroy them".

1. Jericho is presented to us as a city where everyone knew that destruction was coming. The king on his throne knew it, and his most depraved subject knew it also. For forty years they had been aware of a new people, in itself frightened and undisciplined, but moving under the power and direction of its God, Jehovah, and (if we imagine the thoughts of the inhabitants of Jericho), creeping slowly but inexorably across the desert. They had heard about the Red Sea, forty years earlier; they knew about the two kings of the Amorites, so near now in time and place. They knew that Israel's God had given them the land of Canaan, to destroy its inhabitants, and to possess it.

Is not this a picture, true in detail after detail, of the present age and world? Its judgment is surely coming. It has been announced in the Word. It has been ceaselessly proclaimed by the preaching of the Word. Thousands have, like Rahab in her time and place, taken the opportunity the warning provides to secure salvation.

The "wrath to come" was the burden of John Baptist. "Who hath warned you to flee from the wrath to come?" The "wrath to come" is not the last judgment of the great white throne. In the vials containing the seven last plagues is "filled up the wrath of God" (Revelation {15:7,} 16:1). The vials are the final act of destruction before the Coming of Christ in power and glory. It is the time when, to use another figure, He shall "dash them in pieces like a potter's vessel" (Psalm 2:9, N.Tr.). Perhaps the wrath to come on the lips of John Baptist was the destruction of Jerusalem, but in the setting of 1 Thessalonians there can be no question that it is the wrath connected with Christ's Second Advent. God's Son was their Deliverer from the wrath to come.

These thoughts about Jericho and Rahab should certainly stimulate the Christian in his witness, a witness so effectively in operation in Thessalonica as noted just now. The word of the Lord, as witnessed in their faith to God-ward, sounded out in every place, since they themselves had found in God's Son, about to come from heaven, a Deliverer from the "wrath to come". The Lord was speaking to the disciples of the moment, any moment, "when he cometh" that He said, "Let your loins be girded about, and your lights burning". In this world in which we live, the darkness deepens; it is always dark, and thus the disciples are always to have "lights burning".

2. Rahab's confession occupies verses 9-11. Examination of these three verses will direct special attention to four words: "We heard ... I know". "Who hath believed our report" asks the prophet: involved in Rahab's confession is faith in a report heard, a conviction based in the facts reported and accepted. Only thus could she say, "I know". And what was the knowledge confessed? First, "that Jehovah hath given you the land", and then, "Jehovah your God, he is God in heaven above, and in earth beneath". Such a confession, from one nurtured in the religion of Canaan, is most profoundly significant. We are so accustomed to the truth that our God is the sole and sovereign Ruler of heaven and earth, that the extraordinary nature of the new faith now dwelling in Rahab can easily pass us by.

By divine grace and providence, the opportunity, the single great opportunity of her life, presented itself to her by the coming of the spies to her house. She seized it, and came to Jehovah, Israel's God, in the manner in which Boaz described the action of Ruth, "Jehovah, the God of Israel, under whose wings thou art come to trust" (Ruth 2:12).

This faith was manifested by Rahab's acceptance of and action on the promise of the spies, shown in action when she bound the scarlet cord in the window. There was faith also in her whole attitude towards the spies. If Rahab was a corrupt member of a corrupt race, the Israel represented by the spies was a wandering collection of tribes, without home or land, a mysterious horde of nomads born in the desert. Her faith saw them as the people of God before they were manifested as such in Canaan. In this there is a hint of the faith of Moses, "choosing ... to suffer affliction with the people of God", even if in her case, she was escaping the destruction decreed by Israel's God.

If we look for a moment at James 2:25 in the light of verse 21 of the same chapter, we conclude that Rahab already had faith when she received the spies. It is in her *action* of receiving them that she comes before us in James, and the context shows that faith comes before the works there being made prominent.

The *promise* of the spies could only have meaning if two conditions were fulfilled. The first is that the spies must survive. Only if there was living witness in the camp of Israel whence the destruction was imminent could effect be given to the promise. The second is that the eye of the destroyer must light on the scarlet cord. In the glorious gospel of Christ, these two conditions are triumphantly satisfied in the resurrection of the Lord Jesus, in His session in "heaven itself, now to appear in the presence of God for us" (Hebrews 9:24), and in the blood-sprinkled mercy-seat. In the Passover also we see this essential gospel truth: "when I see the blood, I will pass over you".

Perhaps the greatest mark of the action of grace in Rahab's coming to the God of Israel is her place in the genealogy of the Lord Jesus. In Matthew's Gospel (1:3-5) we find a place given in the genealogy to four women; Thamar, Rahab, Ruth and the wife of Urias. None of these would be reckoned, by nature, race or practice, as a candidate for a place when the God of Israel made up beforehand the line of blessing through the Messiah. We have taken account of her brilliant faith to which God responded by putting her in this honoured place in Scripture.

When the Gospel-minded believer in God's use of types and illustrations of New Testament truth in the Old Testament reads the word "scarlet" in connection with the true token in our narrative, he needs no explanation to see suggested in it the scarlet line of salvation through the blood of Christ which runs through Scripture, and ends in the praises of heaven. I have been struck by a sentence in a thoroughly unbelieving author [9] (so far as the

---

[9] J A Soggin, *Joshua: A Commentary*, S.C.M. Press, 1972, page 42

inspiration of the Scripture is concerned): "With regard to the colour of the thread, it reminds me curiously of the blood with which the Israelites in Egypt had to sprinkle the lintels of their doors during the last plague".

3. We can discern some features in the narrative of these chapters, which seem to connect the destruction of Jericho with the judgment of God about to fall on the world. The seven circuits of the city with trumpets cannot but bring to mind the fearful inflictions of the seven trumpets of Revelation 8:7 to 11:15, leading to the seven vials in which is filled up the wrath of God. Whatever we may think and say about the horrors of the Israelite invasion of Canaan, applies with sevenfold force to the period when the wrath of God strikes the world.

In reading these chapters in Joshua, and indeed the whole context of the invasion in the Old Testament history, we cannot but be appalled by the words, so frequently repeated, "utterly destroy". This was not a small event; it was what is called today a genocide. This can be seen most clearly in Deuteronomy 7. "When the Lord thy God shall bring thee into the land whither thou goest to possess it, and hath cast out many nations before thee ... thou shalt smite them, and utterly destroy them; thou shalt [show no] mercy unto them ... ye shall destroy their altars, and break down their images, and cut down their groves, and burn their graven images with fire" (verses 1-5).

To see this genocide in its true light we must first seize the concept of Jehovah, the God of Israel, as the Judge of the nations. God is the Last Judge of all men, and this judgment will appear at the great white throne. But His judgments as Judge of the nations are seen in history, especially Bible history. What lies before us in Joshua is a capital sentence by the righteous and merciful Judge, on the nations inhabiting Canaan. Such a sentence, like any other capital sentence, is as much designed, by perfect love and wisdom, for the preservation of the rest of mankind as for the maintenance of justice. Indeed, the two are inseparable. Large sections of the prophetical Books come into focus for us when we remember the fact of the distinct work of God as the Governor of the nations, as distinct from the last judgment of all the dead (see Isaiah 13 to 23, and Ezekiel 25 to 32).

Two episodes in the life of Abraham connect with these thoughts. In Genesis 15:16 Abram learns that there would be a delay in the accomplishment of the promise to bring Abram's seed into Canaan. In verse 13 we read of four hundred years in Egypt. The reason for the delay is given: "the iniquity of the Amorites is not yet full". By implication, when we arrive at the beginning of the Book of Joshua, then the iniquity of the nations inhabiting Canaan had developed to such a point that the Judge of all the earth must decree extinction. The aspect of merciful preservation by this divine decree for Israel, and indeed for the earth, is seen in Deuteronomy 20:16-18. "Of the cities of these people, which the LORD thy God doth give thee for an inheritance, thou shalt save alive nothing that breatheth: But thou shalt utterly destroy them ... that they teach you not to do after all their abominations, which they have done unto their gods." See also Leviticus 18:25-29. "And the land is defiled; therefore I do visit the iniquity thereof upon it, and the land itself vomiteth out her inhabitants ... Ye shall ... not commit any of these abominations ... that the land spue not you out also ... Therefore shall ye keep mine ordinance, that ye commit not any of these abominable customs".

In Genesis 18:25 we find Abraham appalled at the prospect of the Lord's destruction of the cities of the plain;

but his faith comes to rest in the declaration: "Shall not the Judge of all the earth do right?"

4. Crossing the Jordan

READ JOSHUA 3

It will be helpful at this point to recapitulate. A glance at the second paragraph on page 69, and especially at the Introduction {Chapter 1} to Part 3 on Joshua, would recall to our minds thoughts which provide a good starting point for the present chapter. After a short consideration of some types, we wrote on page 63:

"Here is a justifiable simplification.

1) Canaan, in the earthly history of Joshua, corresponds to 'heavenly places' in the spiritual teaching of Ephesians.

2) The grapes of Eschol, and all the lovely fruits of Canaan, correspond to the 'spiritual blessings' of Ephesians.

3) The fighting to possess Canaan in Joshua corresponds to the Christian's holy war in Ephesians 6:10-18."

The River Jordan was the "mystic barrier" (see page 68) which must be crossed by a people entering Canaan from the wilderness journey. The means of the Christian's entrance into the new life where the spiritual blessings are to be enjoyed lies before us in Ephesians 2:5-6. In verses 1-3 we read that all believers, both Jews and Gentiles, were "by nature the children of wrath ... but God, who is rich in mercy ... even when we were dead in sins, hath *quickened us together with Christ* ... and hath *raised us up together*, and made us *sit together* in heavenly places in Christ Jesus".

Thus, when we read about the exceeding greatness of his power to us-ward, we understand that this power is manifested in two ways. First, in 1:20, it wrought in Christ "when he raised him from the dead, and set him at his own right hand in the heavenly places"; but also secondly, it wrought in us (2:10), in that Christ's quickening has become our quickening; Christ's resurrection has become our resurrection; and the apostle is so bold by the Spirit, as to say that Christ's sitting in the heavenly places has become our sitting in heavenly places. All these facts are facts in the spiritual realm of the heavenly places; and not a jot less real for living than any facts in the natural realm. Thus also we see how just is the view that Jordan, "descending" into the sea of death, represents death, in this connection, the death of One who was once dead on our behalf, on behalf of those who were dead in sins. Worthy art thou, O Lord, "for thou wast slain" for us in Thy mighty love, and art raised from the dead, and art alive for evermore.

At this point we pause to remark that the *purpose* of God for Israel did not include the wilderness journey. His purpose, so frequently made known beforehand, was to bring them out of Egypt and to bring them into Canaan. Having this in view, we might think of the passage of the Red Sea and the crossing of Jordan as coalescing with each other. Possibly they form two parts of one great victory, in which God takes up the people in the slavery in Egypt and places them in the land of Promise.

Viewing the same theme from the standpoint of the New Testament fulfilment, it is vital to see the exact relation between the different epistles, especially Romans and Ephesians, in respect of the believer's death and resurrection with Christ. In Romans we are said to be "crucified with Christ" (6:6), "dead with Christ" (6:8), and "buried with Christ" (6:4). All this *in view of* our walking in newness of life, but the consequences of our union with Christ risen do not in this passage explicitly include anything beyond our being dead with Him. We are at this point seen in His grave with a view to new life and walking in newness of life. In the most notable contrast with this, in Ephesians we have not a word about crucifixion, death or burial with Christ. The apostle's teaching in Ephesian terms finds us in death, since the first consequence of our being united to Christ is our being "quickened with Christ" (2:5). It then goes on to say "raised up together" and "made to sit together" (2:6). In these passages the exact bearing of "quickening" should be observed. It is not, as in today's colloquial speech, a stage in the birth process, but it is, in Scripture, quite exclusively a stage in the resurrection process. This is clearly seen in the usage of the word in the contexts of John 5:21 and 1 Corinthians 15:36. In the resurrection process the first thing needed by the body in the grave is the giving of life, and quickening means just this. Then comes raising into the activities of life.

Just as we have received a hint that we might consider the passage of the Red Sea and the crossing of Jordan as coalescing, so we can now see how the aspects presented in Romans and Ephesians coalesce to form one whole, crucified, dead, buried, quickened, raised and seated in heavenlies with Christ.

When did these six events take place in our experience? The answer is they never did take place in our experience. The Lord Jesus Christ it was who passed through these experiences. Since we were united to Christ in glory by the Holy Spirit sent down from Him in His victory, these events, His death and resurrection are put to our account. We find ourselves sitting, walking and fighting from positions determined by these events – crucifixion, death, and extending through to being raised and seated in heavenly places – passed through by Him. The consequences are experienced by the Christian. The serenity of the sitting, the patience of the walking and the valour of the fighting are brought within our experience since our Joshua is on the throne.

An illustration may be found helpful for seizing these great truths. Consider the case of a child born into a great historic family. The glories and the shame of events in its long and turbulent history were not experienced by the child who now by the simple fact of birth has become an integral part of the family life. The child's own personal experiences are nevertheless to an important degree determined by those events in the history of the family. So, the Christian, alive in a position determined by that succession of events through our Lord Jesus Christ, has passed into the victory and peace of His session at the right hand of God. The child now experiences the happiness (or the misery) belonging to that family life, but its only *experienced* connection with the determining events is – its birth. So the Christian, on hearing and believing the gospel of salvation, and at that moment receiving the Holy Spirit, is made one with Christ in glory, and so is made capable of the feelings which belong to that resurrection life.

All this surely helps us to see how valuable to us is the inspired narrative of the Book of Joshua. It is provided to illustrate and so to bring within the range of our faculties (empowered by the Holy Spirit) the spiritual blessings in the heavenlies set before us in Ephesians. Only those who in Christ have crossed the mystic river and who are on the realised ground of men and women quickened, raised and seated in the heavenlies, can enter into present effective possession of the spiritual blessings[10]. Only such will be able, strong in the Lord, to stand in such possession against the wiles of the devil.

VERSE 1

"They moved from Shittim." This is the first movement of the camp since Numbers 22:1, where we read, "the children of Israel … pitched in the plains of Moab on this side Jordan by Jericho". Shittim was evidently the name of a location at the edge of the plains of Moab, from which the movements described in these chapters took place. Between Shittim and the new encampment on Jordan's banks the whole immense caravan of Israelites scrambled down the steep escarpment between the plateau on which they had encamped so long and the floor of the Jordan Rift at river level. At this time and place the Jordan was a turbulent flood perhaps one mile wide – a formidable barrier indeed.

---

[10] i.e. in their present experience in this life. The believer's election and predestination before the foundation of the world, and his future – "knowing as he is known", and seeing "face to face" – are unconditionally assured to him.

VERSES 2-3

The officers command the people, an enormous host, "When ye see the ark of the covenant of the Lord your God" emerging from the centre of the host borne by the priests, "then ... go after it". In these scenes from Israel's history it is the movements of the ark which determine the movements of the people, and the watchword is, *go after it*. This calls to mind the call of the Lord Jesus to the first disciples, "come ye after me" (Mark 1:17). Likewise in Luke 14:27, with respect to the way of discipleship, "Whosoever doth not bear his cross and come after me, cannot be my disciple". Through these pathways of deep spiritual experience in which the lessons of these chapters must be learned, it is the nearness to the Lord, as he moves before, which is the secret of progress.

VERSE 4

Although the essence of the command in verse 3 was that they must *go after* the ark, a strict limitation on carrying out this command is now imposed. "Come not near unto it." A measured space of one thousand yards was to separate the people from the ark even as they followed it. If the words, *go after it*, find an echo in the call to the disciples, *come after Me*, this space, by which they were to keep their distance from the ark as it passed through Jordan, surely takes us in thought to Gethsemane. There we read that, corresponding to the thousand yards between the ark and the people, there was to be a "stone's cast" between the favoured three disciples and the Lord as he entered into His agony. Read again the story in Mark 14:32-37. "And they came to a place which is called Gethsemane, and he saith to his disciples, Sit ye here while I pray. And he taketh with him Peter and James and John, and began to be sore amazed, and to be very heavy;

And saith unto them, My soul is exceeding sorrowful unto death: tarry ye here and watch. And he went forward a little, and fell on the ground, and prayed that, if it were possible, the hour might pass from him ... And he cometh, and findeth them sleeping, and saith unto Peter, Simon, sleepest thou? couldest not thou watch one hour [with me]?"

Our prayer is that some fresh realisation of the meaning and consequences of the death of Christ for His own may come before us as we ponder the history of the crossing of the Jordan. We can hardly expect this to take place unless we have first of all, and continue to have ever afresh, a realisation of the *fact* of His death. No Scripture presents the totality of the victory gained by the Lord Jesus over death more vividly to us than verse 15 of this chapter, shortly to come before us.

VERSE 7

The passage of Jordan was to take its place alongside that of the Red Sea. These two immense miracles demonstrated the presence of the living God with the hosts of Israel, and also authenticated the mediatorial dignity of Moses and Joshua. "When Israel went out of Egypt, the house of Jacob from a people of strange language: Judah was his sanctuary and Israel his dominion. The sea saw it and fled: Jordan was driven back ... What ailed thee O thou sea, that thou fleddest? thou Jordan, that thou wast driven back? ... Tremble, thou earth, at the presence of the Lord, at the presence of the God of Jacob ..." (Psalm 114).

VERSE 11

The discourse of Joshua to all the people, which occupies verses 9-13, is apparently interrupted by his exclamation,

"Look, the ark ... is moving in front of your eyes into the river".

VERSE 13

There was great faith in the action of Joshua and of the people, in leaving the plateau and descending to take up position at the river's brink. Although the parallel with the drying up of the Red Sea had been noted (2:10), it would appear that this was the first explicit statement that the Jordan would be dried up to permit its passage in dry land.

VERSE 15

"For Jordan overfloweth all his banks all the time of harvest." Doubtless death has always been experienced in widely varying intensities by mankind, though always and only as "the wages of sin". For the Lord Jesus, death was invested with all its terrors. Psalm 22 mightily presents the inmost thoughts and anguish of One suffering death by crucifixion. We can never, never exhaust the utterances which the Lord Jesus addressed to His God at this moment. Every horror attendant on death as the wages of sin was there; hatred, derision, scorn, and mocking of man inspired by Satan – all were there. The "bulls of Bashan", the roaring lion, the encompassing dogs – representing the cruelty of men so animated – were there and thus he was brought "into the dust of death". Yet, beyond all that might have been experienced by "our fathers", there was *His* death – the forsaking by God.

There is a strange echo of these reflections in Jeremiah 12:5. "If in the land of peace, wherein thou trustedst, they wearied thee, then how will thou do in the swelling of Jordan?" This last expression occurs again in Jeremiah 49:19 and 50:44 and also in Zechariah 11:3. In these four instances it is named as the lair of prowling lions. It certainly makes reference to the spate of Jordan during the harvest rains, but appears to connect this with the resulting tropical forests in these areas and the dangers from wild beasts. Is it possible that in the expression, "the swelling of Jordan", indicating a test beyond what man can bear, the Spirit of God really intends a pointer to Psalm 22 and beyond, to the One whose suffering of death formed the basis for the saints' entrance into spiritual blessing according to the counsel of God?

VERSE 17

The subsequent history of Israel in Canaan begins with a formal summary of the leading facts. The priests bearing the ark "stood firm on *dry ground* in the midst of Jordan", and "all the Israelites passed over on *dry ground*". Thus, the ark of Jehovah opened the way and the people of Jehovah were at last on the soil of the promised land.

5. A Solemn Pause

READ JOSHUA 4

In these chapters we find a solemn pause devoted to taking stock, in five important lessons, of the position in which the people of Israel now found themselves. We consider the first two of these in this chapter: the two memorial monuments (4:1-9, 14-24) and the magnifying of Joshua in the sight of Israel (4:14). The other three will be considered in the next chapter.

THE MEMORIAL STONES

The greater part of the narrative of these verses is occupied with the cairn formed from twelve stones lifted "out of the midst of Jordan", out of the place where the priests' feet stood firm, bearing the ark of the covenant. One verse only (4:9) testifies to the erection of a second cairn consisting of twelve different stones set up "in the midst of Jordan, in the place where the feet of the priests which bare the ark stood". The purpose of these monuments is quite specific. The memorial was intended for the children of the future. The exact detail to be impressed on them is very clear also; it was "that the waters of Jordan were cut off" (verse 7), and that "the LORD your God dried up the waters of Jordan" (verse 23).

The memorial aspect of all that has been considered in the previous chapter is vividly presented in Ephesians 2:7; "that in the ages to come he might show the exceeding riches of his grace in his kindness toward us through Christ Jesus". Our thought is naturally drawn by the parallel expression in Ephesians 1:19. The apostle is praying, and comes to the words, "that ye may know ... what is the exceeding greatness of his power to us-ward who believe, according to the working of his mighty power, which he wrought in Christ, when he raised him from the dead, and set him at his own right hand in heavenly places". Here are two expressions to remember, to warm the heart, to cheer the spirit, to calm the soul, to arm for the battle:

- the exceeding greatness of his power

- the exceeding riches of his grace.

The twelve stones so briefly mentioned, set up and submerged in the midst of Jordan speak of something left behind as part of God's victory, at the threshold of an amazing period of victories in Canaan. Certainly what Israel left behind at the entrance to Canaan was the evil heart of unbelief which came out specially when they refused to go forward from Kadesh-Barnea. Before, during the wilderness journey, an endless succession of unbelief, murmuring, disobedience and rejection of God's promise. After, in Canaan, an overall picture of sustained victory. Perhaps these stones correspond to leaving behind the old man, like a rejected garment, according to Ephesians 4:20-24. This casting off refuses place to the devil. This effective rejection accompanies the saints' realisation of their being raised and seated in heavenly places with Christ – exceeding great power of God indeed.

The cairn erected in Gilgal, with its individual stones taken out of Jordan, most assuredly corresponds to individual saints seated in the heavenlies. Grace takes account, not only of the place from which the saints have been taken, but pre-eminently of the limitless range of blessing – the breadth, length, depth and height – God had in view in taking them up. Let us pause and take account of this fact, that true riches, real wealth are to be found in Ephesian truth regarding God, Christ and the saints – the true Canaan. Oh may the vision of such wealth, in the glory that excelleth, outshine everything of earth and the world, even as the sun outshines the stars!

An extremely suggestive phrase occurs separately with reference to both sets of twelve memorial stones: "the place where". Regarding the stones taken out of the river (4:3) we read "Take you hence out of the midst of Jordan, out of *the place where* the priests' feet stood firm". Dealing with the stones to be set up in the middle and submerged in the river (4:9) it says "Joshua set up twelve stones in the midst of Jordan, in *the place where* the feet of the priests ... stood". Certainly to myself this immediately brings to mind, "He is not here: for he is risen, as he said. Come, see *the place where* the Lord lay" (Matthew 28:6). We shall never, never see with understanding and truly enlightened eyes the transcendent fullness of Christ at God's right hand, unless ever and again there flows over our spirits in remembrance the death with all its terrors where Jesus once stood in His great love, on our behalf. Is it not to this end that perfect wisdom and love has ordained the Lord's Supper?

JOSHUA MAGNIFIED

The Lord had promised Joshua that in the events of this day He would increase the stature of Joshua in the eyes of all Israel. The fulfilment of this promise is given in 4:14:

"on that day the LORD magnified Joshua in the sight of all Israel: and they feared him, as they feared Moses, all the days of his life". So far as effective command over the people is concerned Joshua was given the stature of Moses (Moses remains unique, of course, in his nearness to God). It is obvious that a major element in the days of victory which lay ahead for Israel was the leadership of Joshua; and the quality which takes this leadership out of the realm of mere human abilities, is that it consisted in Joshua's mediation in giving the word of the Lord for every occasion. The effect of this on Israel's enemies is wonderfully seen in Balaam's prophecy concerning the wandering nomads whose tents lay before Balak: "Jehovah is with him, and the shout of a king is among them".

In taking up the comparison between the crossings of the Red Sea and of Jordan under Moses and Joshua respectively, there are differences appropriate to each. But the essential feature was that Joshua committed himself beforehand in the ears of all the people to the word of the Lord. The instant the first Israelite feet touched the waters of Jordan, then Jehovah would intervene with a mighty miracle directed to the guarantee that *the living God* was among them, and therefore He would drive before Israel the terrifying Canaanites with giants and walled cities. This was precisely what Joshua and Caleb had maintained against the other spies: "If the LORD delight in us, then he will bring us into this land, and give it to us" {Numbers 14:8}.

No Old Testament worthy has a claim stronger than Joshua's to be recognised as representing Christ. That the names, Joshua and Jesus are identical is seen in Acts 7:45 and Hebrews 4:8. In the latter case especially such use of the name Jesus is very natural and fitting. The writer had the Septuagint in front of him, the Greek Old Testament, and was in the middle of a series of exact quotations from it. What more natural than to continue his quotations by using the Septuagint name for Israel's leader in Canaan? And so Joshua is before us very expressly as representing Christ Himself.

The apostle Paul has often moved our hearts deeply by his word in the face of death by martyrdom: "my earnest expectation and hope ... that ... Christ shall be magnified in my body, whether it be by life, or by death". From such a man, by the same Holy Spirit, we have in Ephesians 1 words directed to magnifying our Joshua in the eyes of all the saints. He does this by fixing our gaze on Christ where He is now, at God's own right hand. Let us take that long look! I mean long, not in the number of words used, but in the time we allow ourselves at this moment to make good use of the eyes mentioned in verse 18: eyes of our heart, eyes enlightened by God.

It is a familiar experience, if not often described, that, on moving from surroundings brilliantly illuminated into dim light, one experiences a fleeting instant of blindness. In some diseases of the eye this period of blindness is lengthened. This thing is a parable. We pass our days of normal awareness in the brilliant light of earthly things. More than the fleeting moment required for reading these words is required if we are to receive a deep and lasting impression of the greatness of that glorious Man who is in a world whose brightness is too often dimmed by the light of earthly things, if He is truly to be magnified in our eyes, as we see Him in heaven's light. It is a question to be asked: has *meditation* any place at all in our lives? Without it our eyes will not penetrate the veil of time and sense. Let us heed the word: let us set our mind on things above by taking time for meditation: for it is there we find Christ sitting at the right hand of God.

The splendid position given to the raised and ascended Christ is the theme when the words occur, "His body, the fullness of Him that filleth all in all" (Ephesians 1:23). Are we about to be told that principalities and powers are the powerful enemies of the saints? Are there great names of "wisdom, love and power" borne by men and angels? Christ is far above them all. With the Greeks, the expression "all things" was a technical term for the universe, and there was perpetual speculation about its nature and destiny. The universe is under His feet: and He fills it.

That Christ fills all things has been likened to the sun filling the solar system with its warmth and light. Another illustration preserves the idea of a Man and His world. One of the greatest names named in the world of the New Testament is that of Augustus (compare Luke 2:1). This great man was the architect of the Roman Empire, which gave the majesty of the Roman peace to the world in a system which endured for half a millennium. Many emperors were of course evil men but in his own day there was no corner of the inhabited earth which did not enjoy in good measure the fruits of the wisdom, mercy and power of Augustus. So, lifting the illustration out of its connection with sinful man, when the glories of Christ fill the universe, there will be no corner of it where His wisdom, love and power in all their divine perfection, will not be a living reality: and this is the glorious Person with whom the saints are united in His body which is the church.

6. A Solemn Pause (continued)

READ JOSHUA 5

Circumcision, the old corn of the land, the Man with the drawn sword: what lessons have these evocative phrases for us? In this chapter that question is answered from the teaching of the New Testament epistles.

In my last chapter two events of the "solemn pause" that followed the Israelites' passage of the Jordan were studied – the two sets of memorial stones and the magnifying of Joshua. Three other events preceded the besieging of Jericho. They are recorded in the fifth chapter and we turn to them now.

CIRCUMCISION REINSTITUTED

The first institution of circumcision, given to Abraham as the seal of the covenant, is found in Genesis 17. In Gilgal, "the LORD said to Joshua, 'Make thee sharp knives, and circumcise again the children of Israel the second time'" (5:2). This second institution had for its purpose to "roll away the reproach of Egypt from off" them (verse 9), and an immediate preparation for the battles ahead.

A careful perusal of verses 4 to 9 brings out a pre-occupation with Egypt. The "reproach of Egypt"

A SOLEMN PAUSE

consisted in the fact that it was the men who came out of Egypt who rebelled against God at Kadesh in refusing to proceed with the possession of Canaan. Gilgal signalised the fact that these had been "consumed" (verse 6). It was a silent but urgent stimulus to courage for the battle. In us believers it is the flesh explicitly which is "not subject to the law of God nor indeed can be" (Romans 8:7). If we take note of how God has dealt with the flesh we shall see in a moment the application of Gilgal to ourselves.

If we consider afresh the position of Israel at Gilgal, then it is easy to see that the remembrance of those men who had been consumed in the forty years' wandering would be salutary not only as regards the actual "consuming", but also against Israel's confidence in themselves. This is exactly where the true meaning of circumcision brings the Christian. "We are the circumcision, which ... have no confidence in the flesh" (Philippians 3:3). This is the point at which we must look more carefully at the New Testament teaching about the application in Christianity of the "type" of circumcision.

First, in Romans 2:28-29, we learn that the ultimate circumcision is in the heart and spirit, not in the body. In other words, God had in mind from the beginning the meaning and application of circumcision to the Christian. Next, we learn from Colossians 2:10-11. The real circumcision is reckoned to the Christian from the moment of faith, when he is united to Christ in glory (verse 10). The circumcision with which the Christian is circumcised is exactly defined: "putting off the body of ... the flesh, by the circumcision of Christ". In the context His circumcision can only mean His death. In no sense has the Christian living on this earth put off the body of flesh and blood; therefore "the body" in the text can only mean its totality. The "putting off" is constantly renewed by the Christian, as is typified in this reinstitution and in the return to Gilgal after each victory. But finally we revert to the connotation of circumcision in Philippians 3:3. "We are the circumcision, who worship by the Spirit of God, and boast in Christ Jesus, and do not trust in flesh" (N.Tr.).

"No confidence in flesh" is tremendously strengthened by turning back to Joshua 5:2. "Make thee *sharp knives* and circumcise". If swords are to be victorious in battle against Canaanites, sharp knives must be made and turned on self. How much that is so slack and spineless about the Christianity of today is due to lack in, or total absence of, work with the sharp knives? Is this application to be found in scripture? Explicitly and abundantly! "If thy right hand be a snare to thee, cut it off" (Matthew 5:30, N.Tr.). The Saviour's words speak not of the physical body, of course, but of the mind and spirit; still one's flesh shudders in the contemplation of the picture conjured up by them. They urge upon us what we ought to be doing. "If we would judge ourselves, we should not be judged" (1 Corinthians 11:31). "If we confess our sins, he is faithful and just to forgive us our sins, and to cleanse us from all unrighteousness" (1 John 1:9). "Put to death, therefore, your members which are upon the earth, fornication, uncleanness, vile passions, ... wrath, anger, malice" (Colossians 3:5, 8; N.Tr.). It was said to me long ago, alas, often forgotten, "Most people find all the excuses for themselves, and are strict with others. Be as tolerant as you can with the faults of others; be tough with yourself."

THE CORN OF THE LAND

In preparation for battles, the indispensability of assuring food supplies was asserted by Napoleon in the famous, if ambiguous sentence, "An army marches on its stomach".

The needs of the wilderness wanderings had been supplied by the miracle of the manna. It comes as something of a shock to realise that, unmentioned, the manna had continued all along the King's highway, past the plains of Moab, and into the land of Canaan as far as Gilgal. And it was so with the corn of the land. They both slipped into the silence of familiar routine. This is, of course, only one aspect of the maintenance of food supplies. Other aspects of the history forbid the allowance of the contempt bred by familiarity, but unless the assuring of the Christian's spiritual food becomes a thing of fixed habit, the fight will not be sustained, and we shall not be found, "having done all", standing (Ephesians 6:13).

The type of the manna is most emphatically interpreted by the Lord Jesus in John's Gospel chapter 6. Five times it is repeated that He was Himself, in His own Person, the true bread "which cometh down from Heaven" (John 6:33, 38, 42, 51, 58); and this in the context of verses 31-32. "Our fathers did eat manna in the desert ... bread from heaven". The manna is the Lord Jesus Himself, as food for the soul, as the One come down from heaven to be food and life for His people in the desert. The corn of the land is, in the light of this word of the Lord Jesus, not difficult to interpret. It is the Lord Jesus Himself in glory, in that heaven to which He belongs, where is His eternal home, and this to be His people's food to give strength for the battles of their holy war.

It would appear that, of the solemn pause we are considering in this chapter, three successive days are found in these verses (5:10-12). Israel kept the Passover on the fourteenth day of the month (verse 10): they ate the corn of the land of Canaan on the fifteenth (verse 11): and the manna ceased on the sixteenth (verse 12).

There can be no question about the application of the Passover and Unleavened Bread to the Christian life. It is clearly explained and powerfully applied in 1 Corinthians 5:7 and 8: "Purge out therefore the old leaven, that ye may be a new lump, as ye are unleavened. For even Christ our passover is sacrificed for us: Therefore let us keep the feast, not with old leaven, neither with the leaven of malice and wickedness; but with the unleavened bread of sincerity and truth". Regarding the character and behaviour which prepared for the fight, let us notice the parallels between the passage just quoted and Ephesians chapter four: "truth" is urged upon us in verses 15, 21 and 24: and the casting off of "malice" in verse 31.

In the narrative of the first Passover in Egypt and in the regulations for the Feasts of Jehovah, eating of the slain lamb and of unleavened bread are most closely joined together. A person who started to eat the passover committed himself to eating unleavened bread. Thus the Christian who gets the blessing from the blood of God's Lamb, is committed for life to the kind of living of 1 Corinthians 5:8.

Coming now to verse 11, and the "corn of the land", Israel's eating it corresponds to the Christian's feeding, mind, heart and spirit, on the Lord Jesus; but now it is in a special character and position. It is Christ in heaven. He came down from heaven, and is now in heaven. It is His own place, to which He belongs. This is a most important distinction in faith and in practice. That is only real Christianity which centres on Christ in heaven. J. B. Stoney said, "A person will often say, 'I stick only to Christ' without any thought going beyond His earthly life, and not centring on Christ in heaven". For our struggle in the heavenlies as described in Ephesians chapter six, we need to feed on Christ in heaven. What wealth of teaching is available to us concerning Christ now in heaven! This is not the place or time to expound the truths; we can only give a lead as to what they are and where they are to be found.

A very special case is that of the epistle to the Hebrews, deeply founded in the books of the law available to Joshua. The moment when the High Priest enters into the holiest with the blood of sacrifice is pinpointed to be the theme of the epistle: Christ entered into the very presence of God, and seated at the right hand of God is the source from which all the blessings of that epistle flow. Most particularly pertinent to our theme in Joshua, of course, is the present position, grace and activity of Christ at God's right hand as Lord and Head. To direct our attention to such a Person, and in such a position is a main purpose of the types in Joshua. These thoughts lead very naturally to the final paragraph of our theme.

THE CAPTAIN OF THE LORD'S HOST

In the first three of these lessons the attention of Joshua and the host of Israel was directed to remembering the lessons of the *past*. In the fourth, *present* action still recalled the contrasts with the past. In this fifth paragraph Joshua is bidden to attend to the *future* wars.

One thing further is needed before actual warfare commences and it seems to be Joshua himself who needs it, for it was given to him alone to see it, and we have no record of its being passed on to the people. It is implied that Joshua was alone, surveying the city in secret, and perhaps dismayed before the immensity of the enterprise about to begin? He became aware of something unusual, looked around, and there stood a man, naked sword in hand!

We are soon aware that this is a theophany – an appearance of God. Since God is known in Christ, we might say that it is an appearance of Christ. Other theophanies had gone before, and others were to follow. The two theophanies in earlier books are the three men who appeared to Abram (Genesis 18) and the burning bush (Exodus 3:2). Regarding the former, there is a striking difference between the character of the men who appeared to Abram and that of Him who appeared to Joshua. To Abram the pilgrim there came peaceful travellers, accepting the courtesies due to travellers, and communing with him about his future. Now, to Joshua, Jehovah appears, not as a peaceful traveller, but as a warrior, ready for immediate fighting. This is the first part of the lesson: Jehovah is a warrior.

The second part of the lesson is in the answer to Joshua's question, "Art thou for us, or for our adversaries?" The answer refuses the question, as much as to say, "Adversaries are nothing, non-existent, if you learn the lesson that this war is My war, and you are My army". The word translated "host" sometimes means "Heavenly bodies" and sometimes "angels". The context here is plainly in favour of "army". "As captain of the host of the LORD am I now come". Joshua was Israel's leader, appointed by Jehovah, and already magnified in the people's eyes. But Joshua was that invincible leader required by the promises only inasmuch as in complete obedience to Jehovah he faithfully mediated Jehovah's word and power. The real captain is Jehovah.

At this point a simple reading in Ephesians 6:12 will serve to confirm vividly where the New Testament counterpart of the conquest of Canaan is to be found. Note particularly the strong implication that the apostle Paul has in mind some *other* struggle, but then against human foes, which nevertheless forms an instructive parallel to the struggle he now describes:

"For we wrestle not against flesh and blood, but against principalities, against powers ... against spiritual wickedness in heavenly places" (compare AV margin). In terms of the conflict for the spiritual blessings in heavenly places no doubt it is Christ in glory as Head who, through the believer's union with Him, is the supplier of all that is needed for every aspect of life (Ephesians 1:22 and 4:8). But can there be any real doubt that the "Captain of the Lord's host" in Joshua 5 is a clear pointer to Ephesians 6:10 – "Finally my brethren, be strong in the Lord, and in the power of his might"?

We now turn for a moment to consider the theophany of the burning bush, and to compare it with that of the Captain of the Lord's host. Whereas it is the contrasts that are instructive when comparing the latter with the theophany to Abram, this time it is the parallels. Some of these can be seen in the Table.

JOSHUA 5		EXODUS 3, ETC.	
5:13	looked and behold	3:2	looked and behold
5:14	the host of the LORD	7:4	mine armies [hosts]
		12:41	the hosts of the LORD
5:14	am I now come	3:8	I am come down
5:15	Loose thy shoe from off thy foot; for the place whereon thou standest is holy	3:5	Put off thy shoes from off thy feet, for the place whereon thou standest is holy ground

JOSHUA 5		EXODUS 3, ETC.	
5:6	the land which the LORD sware unto their fathers ... that floweth with milk and honey	3:8	to bring them unto a land flowing with milk and honey.
5:12	they did eat of the fruit of the land of Canaan that year	3:8	to bring them ... unto the place of the Canaanites

We have previously had occasion to compare the meaning of the Red Sea passage with the crossing of the Jordan and to see them coalesce to form one whole view of the putting into effect of God's purpose, taking up Israel in Egypt and placing them in Canaan. Perhaps the two appearances of Jehovah, in the burning bush and as Captain of the Lord's host – as compared in the Table – coalesce in a similar way, tending to present redemption from Egypt and establishment in Canaan as two sides of one event. The great lesson repeated and received with such solemnity is that no victory is possible that does not fully square with God's holiness.

By this time we would expect Joshua and Ephesians each to illuminate the message of the other. It is certainly so in this case. The section of Ephesians giving general exhortations, as distinct from special relationships, runs from 4:17 to 5:21. In the early portion of this section, we have a reference to the warfare of chapter 6, in that it pinpoints the kind of behaviour which gives victory to the devil; "let not the sun go down upon your wrath: neither give place to the devil" (Ephesians 4:26-27). Close by, in this same portion, we find holiness put in as the behaviour which tends to victory; "having put on the new man, which according to God is created in truthful righteousness and holiness" (4:24, N.Tr.), and "Do not grieve the Holy Spirit of God" (4:30, N.Tr.). In the fighting which so soon ensued, the *only* defeat suffered by Israel in pitched battle was after Achan had sinned in the accursed thing. Let the last terse words of the chapter remain with us: "And Joshua did so".

7. The Walls of Jericho

READ JOSHUA 6

The walls which protected one of Satan's strongholds in the land of promise, and the apparently powerless, but obedient, procedure which caused their collapse, have direct lessons for the believer who seeks "to make his position his possession".

The most striking sentences in chapter six are: "and the walls of the city shall fall down flat" (verse 5), "the walls fell down flat" (verse 20).

Did anyone recall the report of the first spies from the wilderness which so frightened Israel? "The cities are walled and very great", "The cities are very great and walled up to heaven" (Numbers 13:28 and Deuteronomy 1:28). Our first study will consider the means employed to bring about this decisive victory. What were the weapons of Israel's warfare? They were trumpets, shouting, faith and obedience.

The nature of the trumpets warrants careful study. The kind of trumpet found in Joshua 6, at Sinai, for the year of "jubilee", and frequently as a battle call or alarm, is the "*shophar*". The word "*jobel*" is translated in AV either "jubilee" or "ram's horn", but better, means "a loud noise" or "shouting". It is connected with alarm, rejoicing or terror. The context decides which. Lastly there is the "*chatsotserah*" (see Appendix: The Sound of the Silver Trumpets), a trumpet which in Numbers 10 was made of silver, and was used for movement commands, for alarm or with singing. The emphasis here is on a clear sound, and hence on a clear command. This characteristic is in sharp contrast with the loud noise or "*jobel*".

The characteristic of usage in Joshua 6 is that "*shophar*" and "*jobel*" come together five times (verses 4, 5, 6, 8, 13) the phrase being translated in AV "trumpets of ram's horns", but more accurately "trumpets of loud noise". The only other case in which these two words come together is at Sinai (Exodus 19) and this passage determines the meaning in context:

> Exodus 19:16: "there were thunders and lightnings and a thick cloud upon the mount, and the voice of the trumpet exceeding loud; so that all the people that was in the camp trembled".

> 19:19{, 24}: "And when the voice of the trumpet sounded long, and waxed louder and louder, Moses spake and God answered him by a voice ... let not the priests and the people break through to come up unto the LORD lest he break forth upon them".

The trumpets in Joshua then are by context "trumpets of loud noise", noise of terror witnessing the presence of Jehovah in destruction. Jericho was rather less than one hundred and fifty yards across, and therefore such trumpet blasts would be heard across the city, reaching every corner.

It was in fact the shout which brought down the walls. Six days the host encircled the city once each day, and for those days Joshua said, "Ye shall not shout, nor make any noise with your voice ... until the day I bid you shout; then shall ye shout" (verse 10). And so they did: "when the people heard the sound of the trumpet, and the people shouted with a great shout, the wall fell down flat, so that the people went up into the city, every man straight before him, and they took the city". Trumpet and shout come together again in 1 Thessalonians 4:16, "the Lord himself shall descend from heaven with a shout, with the voice of the archangel, and the trump of God: and the dead in Christ shall rise first". Also the number seven is central in the account of the trumpet's sounding in the Revelation 8:2 to 11:15. All this prepares us for the understanding that here in our chapter we have what symbolises in some sense the destruction of the world and the entrance of the people of God into blessing. The shout witnessed Israel's certainty of victory.

In Hebrews 11:30 we learn that it was "by faith the walls of Jericho fell down after they were compassed about seven days". Just as in the previous verses of Hebrews 11 we can see the faith of Moses and separately the faith of the people at the departure from Egypt and the keeping of the Passover, so here we can see both the faith of Joshua in commanding the people and the faith of the people in acting as they did. Faith is manifested by action. When people do what God says, then faith must be in action.

And so the great central weapon in the panoply of Israel in this first, but decisive encounter with the armies and kings of Canaan is obedience to the word of God. The fact that these weapons would be foolishness in the eyes of the watchers from the walls of Jericho was not a factor in determining events.

A review of the history of Israel in scripture reveals that from the wilderness journey to the final extinction of the kingdoms of Israel and Judah, the constant theme of the prophets is God's judgment coming because of disobedience. They always failed to maintain what God commanded, and always did the things He forbade. The Book of Joshua is unique in this respect – a very striking history of unbroken obedience. After the serious lapse of one man here at Jericho, there is unbroken obedience, and – marvellous witness to God's power and faithfulness to His word and promise – unbroken victory. The defeat at Ai, and the moral defeat by the "wiles" of the enemy at Gibeon are searching lessons in their place. Oh for ears today to hearken to the message of this unique example of obedience and its power!

It is time we returned to consider the great teaching of this book for the Christian – the Christian's warfare in heavenly places. What, in this application, corresponds to this celebrated event, "the walls fell down flat"?

This wall was a defensive structure for the king of Jericho and his armed forces. It aimed to prevent the destruction of the accursed race, and thus to hinder Israel from possessing its possessions. Very precise light is available at this point in 2 Corinthians 10:4-5. "For the weapons of our warfare are not carnal, but mighty through God to the pulling down of strongholds; casting down imaginations, and every high thing that exalteth itself against the knowledge of God, and bringing into captivity every thought to the obedience of Christ". One hears surprisingly little attention paid to this very striking passage. In it we have "weapons" and "warfare" – "strongholds" and "high things lifted up" (walls, in other words). The result of victory is "obedience", and all is in the realm of thought and spirit – "imaginations" or reasonings, and "every thought". Paul had not been able to occupy the Corinthian saints with the mystery, the precious things available to the believer in heavenly places, because an enormous thought barrier existed in them. In the realm of spirit and thought they were carnal. There loomed large in the thought and spirit "the wisdom of the world", "envying and strife", all things hostile to the destruction of the accursed thing, and to the knowledge of God. Some of our most cherished thoughts and reasonings could enter into the material forming "the wall".

And so the king of Jericho and all his forces are locked up and protected from destruction by this wall. The last we read of the king of Jericho is verse 2; "I have given into thine hand Jericho, and the king thereof, and the mighty men of valour". Allusion has been made to the destruction of the world, and this thought that the destruction of the world is in some sense symbolised here is supported by two references in Ephesians. In 2:2 the theme is the past life for the Ephesian believers; they "walked according to the course of this world, according to the prince of the power of the air, the spirit that now worketh in the children of disobedience". Also 6:12 with explicit reference to the Christian's warfare in heavenly places; "we wrestle not against flesh and blood [as Israel did], but against (spiritual authorities), against the rulers of the darkness of this world, against spiritual wickedness in high [heavenly] places". Looking over the enemies of Israel throughout her history, the king of Egypt represents the world in keeping Israel under slavery in Egypt. The kings of the Amorites and Canaanites aimed to keep Israel out of the land of promise. Later, the king of Babylon removed them from their land of promise because of disobedience. Thus we have here in Jericho and its king one aspect of the many-sided opposition of the world animated in the spiritual realm by Satan. The Christian meets this opposition directly in his own spirit, if his aim is to *stand* in possession of the experiences of knowledge and understanding (Ephesians 1:17-18) of the indwelling of Christ and the comprehension of the love of Christ which passeth knowledge (Ephesians 3:16-21). A first exercise awakened by these thoughts from scripture is to question our hearts whether we are over on Christ's side of things in spirit. Or are our exercises confined to achieving serenity in daily cares or success in the service of God, both basically self-centred? These latter experiences are of very great importance in the eyes of the Lord, but he wants us active and exercised and praying to be in line with the purpose of God's grace for us.

Our thoughts on the victory in heavenly places must have two sides; first, the once-for-all victory of Christ for us, and second, the saints' victory in the conflict of Ephesians 6. We have just spoken of the latter, and, thanks be to God, the Word is clear as to the former. In the same section of Ephesians as that just quoted we must pinpoint that stage in the victory of Christ to which our previous meditations on the Book of Joshua have brought us, that is, the ascension of Christ (on page 87). We cannot be confirmed too strongly in this, as in all other aspects of Christ's victory. The ascension in this connection comes before us in Ephesians 1:20-30 and 4:8-10. We have all along laid great stress on "the exceeding greatness of his power" in the ascended Christ at God's right hand, and on "the exceeding riches of his grace" (1:19 and 2:7). Let us now reflect a little on 4:8. It is when ascended upon high, having gotten the victory, that He dispenses the fruits of His victory for the equipment of the saints for their work of service; and this equipment includes all they need, for all the time they need it, to make them overcomers in the war.

In the movements of the armed men, the priests and the people, their actions, extending to the trumpet blasts and the shout, carried out in minute obedience to the Lord's commands, mediated the power of God for the entrance of His people into possession of Canaan. The essential of these movements was the bearing and the display of the ark, mentioned nine times in the chapter. J. G. Bellett has a striking passage[11]:

"A mere journey from Egypt to Canaan would not have constituted true pilgrimage. Many a one had travelled that road without being a stranger and pilgrim with God. ... A merely toilsome, self-denying life, even though endued with that moral courage which becomes God's strangers on earth, will not do. In order to make that journey the journey of God's Israel, the *ark* must be in their company, borne by a people ransomed by blood out of Egypt, and tending, in their faith of a promise, to Canaan. ... And what ark is in the midst of the saints now for safe and holy and honourable conduct through the desert world, if not the name of the Son of God? What mystery is committed to our stewardship and testimony, if not that? 'He that abideth in the doctrine of Christ, he hath both the Father and the Son. If there come any unto you, and bring not this doctrine, receive him not into your house, neither bid him God speed'. The wall of partition is to be raised by the saints between them and Christ's dishonour."

[11] J G Bellett, *The Son of God*, London: W H Broom, 1869, pages 2-3

This people, moving round Jericho, possessed the emblem of Jehovah's presence with them: every detail of their action centred around this fact. The church consists of a people amongst whom is known in faith the precious mystery of the Person of the Son of God, "the eternal Son of the eternal Father", now ascended up on high, and seated at God's right hand. The trumpets and the shout represent witness to this, made effective in the detail of the obedience.

What exactly is the nature of the obedience portrayed here? I think we get more than an hint on this in "the whole armour of God" (Ephesians 6:13). Having read so far through the Ephesian Epistle, we might have conditioned our thought to expect that the putting on of the armour would consist in some tremendous transaction in the purely spiritual realm. Not so: the armour consists in truth, righteousness, peace, salvation, the word of God and prayer. I think, therefore, that it is obedience in the whole detail of life in the world, the family and the church which releases the victory power in this purely spiritual realm. Women, with heads covered in church, in obedience whether they understand or not, are a sight which has effects among these same spiritual powers.

It has just been remarked that in the struggle of Ephesians 6:12 the spiritual energy put out by hostile powers in the spiritual realm acts directly on the believer's spirit. We are here learning that it is in lives in which is enshrined in the inward sense the confessed knowledge of the Son of God, seated at God's right hand, lives lived in the outward sense in obedience to God's word in every detail of life, that the power of Christ's victory over principalities and powers (Colossians 2:15) is released. "Now unto him [the Father] that is able to do exceeding abundantly above all we ask or think, according to the power that worketh in us, to him be glory in the church through Christ Jesus throughout all ages, world without end. Amen" (Ephesians 3:20-21).

It remains to look at verses 17-19. These verses present types of most serious and urgent practical questions. In section 3 of Chapter 3, on pages 82 to 84, we looked in a preliminary way at the fearful action in 6:21 and 24: "and they utterly destroyed all that was in the city, both man and woman, young and old, and ox and sheep, and ass, with the edge of the sword. ... And they burnt the city with fire, and all that was therein; only the silver and the gold, and the vessels of brass and of iron, they put into the treasury of the house of the LORD". In that place our conclusion was that our faith, like Abraham's, can only come to rest in "shall not the Judge of all the earth do right?"

Now we must look more closely at this aspect of the inspired narrative. First, notice the adjective in the phrases, "the accursed thing", "the city shall be accursed" (three times in verse 17 and verse 18), and also the verb in verse 21. These are forms from the same root which means "to set apart for God". The action applies to "the city and everything in it". But this setting apart was carried out in two ways. The persons were to be put to the sword and then all perishable things burned with fire. The imperishable things were to be put into the treasury of the Lord's house (the tabernacle). It is clear therefore that the reason for this fearful sentence, carried out throughout this conquest, was that the detestable practices which filled the Canaanite religion required that everything Canaanite must be removed from human circulation. Perishables were to cease to exist by being burned; imperishable things were, so to speak, to revert to the original control of the Creator.

118

There can be little doubt where we shall find the analogous ban in the Christian's warfare in heavenly places. We take up the thread from Chapter 6, on page 108, which brought us to Ephesians in the section 4:17 to 5:21. More precisely now, we find in 5:3-7 what unmistakeably corresponds to the detestable practices associated with Canaanite religion. It is in the parallel passage in Colossians 3:5-7 that we encounter exactly the parallel of the ban in Joshua 6:17-19; "mortify", kill, put to death: "Mortify therefore your members which are upon the earth; fornication, uncleanness, inordinate affection, evil concupiscence, and covetousness, which is idolatry; for which things' sake the wrath of God cometh on the children of disobedience: in the which ye also walked sometime, when ye lived in them". Let the mature Christian note, as well as the young disciple, that none ever gets beyond the solemn warnings and commands of these passages.

The reason for these appalling measures is found in verse 18. If they were disobedient in this respect, then the people of Israel, and the camp itself would become also devoted to destruction. The story of Achan in the next chapter follows so sadly from this verse.

8. The Valley of Achor

READ JOSHUA 7:1 TO 8:29

Like the Scripture Truth *editor of the original of this chapter, readers will find it searching and humbling. Self-exposure under the Word of God is one of the prime ways in which it helps us.*

The events described in these two chapters are uniquely important for the understanding of the narrative and its application to the Christian. The reason for this statement is simple. The defeat at Ai was the only defeat on the field of battle suffered by the forces of Israel in all the campaigns of the book of Joshua. Moreover, the statement acquires special emphasis from a consideration of casualties. The thirty-six Israelites "smitten" by the men of Ai were the only casualties suffered by Israel in all these campaigns. Not a single death in battle is recorded. What could be achieved at the level of victory in battles on the single and simple basis of obedience in strategy and tactics is without limit; and for the people of God in every dispensation, from beginning to end of the Book of God, no lesson is more important than this – "to obey is better than sacrifice".

VERSE 1

As the narrative passes from chapter six to the opening of chapter seven, all seemed set fair for the progress and success of the enterprise to take possession of the land of Canaan. The opening verse of the new chapter abundantly justifies the huge capitals with which the English Versions generally emphasise the first word. With the tremendous BUT, the verse stands alone in any analysis of the chapter. "But the children of Israel committed a trespass in the accursed thing; for Achan ... took of the accursed thing: and the anger of the LORD was kindled against the children of Israel." The action was Achan's; and perhaps the genealogy suggests influences lying behind the action; but the consequences lay upon the whole of the people. The verse reveals the one thing of real consequence in any situation – the state of affairs as seen under the eye of God, before a single move is made in that action. Could Israel have been aware of this? It is difficult to avoid the conclusion that they could. If they had enquired of the Lord, He would have revealed it.

Since we have in this verse the principles underlying defeat, very careful study is appropriate so that we may learn its lessons for ourselves. It fixes attention on sin in the heart and life of believers, and therefore in the church: on its effect, discovery, and the urgency of immediate action to deal with it according to God. It would not be possible to command the attention of readers with an exhaustive treatment of the matter, but I beseech the reader to read the following passages with the closest attention: Matthew 15:19; Galatians 5:19-21; Ephesians 5:3, 5; Colossians 3:5-6; 1 Corinthians 5:11, 13; Matthew 5:27-30 (especially verse 30). We must try, as tersely as possible, to draw out the implications of Joshua 7 for the Christian's warfare in heavenly places.

1) The flesh is present in the believer, and in the wisdom and love of God will continue with us during our earthly life. In the cross and the Spirit are the means of victory, and there is no condemnation attached to the presence of the flesh in the believer. It is at the precise point where lusts after the *gratification* of the flesh manifest themselves that action – immediate, vigorous, ruthless – is demanded.

2) In the church epistles there are three lists of sins, and attached to them the sternest rejection. Two, typical because they are found in all such lists, are fornication and covetousness, which is idolatry. I shall try to show, by examination of the context of each, that they qualify explicitly for acceptance as the sins pictured in "the accursed thing" of our chapter.

   (a) Ephesians 5:3-6. Compare verse 6 with verse 1 of our chapter in Joshua: "because of these things cometh the wrath of God upon the children of disobedience" and "the anger of the LORD was kindled against the children of Israel". Notice also Joshua 1:6 "for unto this people shalt thou divide for an inheritance the land". In later chapters the word 'inheritance' is especially characteristic of this book.

   (b) Colossians 3:5. "Mortify (put to death) therefore your members which are upon the earth", and the verse goes on to identify "your members" with the sins listed. This verse and this action is most vividly illustrated in Matthew 5:30 "If thy right hand offend thee, cut it off, and cast it from thee: for it is profitable for thee that one of thy members should perish ...".

(c) 1 Corinthians 5:11, 13. The same sins are listed here, and in the context of 1 Corinthians, demand excommunication, no less. This demonstrates as nothing else could the need for total exclusion of these offences. Nevertheless I cannot believe that excommunication is the lesson of Achan in Israel for us. The former is exclusion with a view to restoration of the individual. The latter is total destruction of the "members" responsible for the sin, and in each case must be worked out in and by each for himself. This is true in spite of the fact that the whole company is involved. To this we now turn.

(d) In the first verse of our chapter, a notable point to observe is that the guilt and the anger of Jehovah, rests on all Israel. This we see in church epistles in the New Testament.

1 Corinthians 5:6, indicating that in case (c) above, the whole assembly is involved. "A little leaven leaveneth the whole lump".

Galatians 5:9, the same words, in this case connected with errors of doctrine. There is an interesting echo of our chapter in Galatians 1:7 and 5:12, if we recall that Achan and Achor mean 'trouble'. "I would that they were even cut off which trouble you."

VERSES 2-5

All unaware of Achan's sin and of the disaster entailed by it, Joshua made his dispositions for assault on the next city, a small one. Here also there was a large 'but'. Joshua himself was at fault at this stage. He did not enquire of Jehovah. He went forward on the crest of the wave of appearances straight into disaster. And this disaster had its causes entirely in Israel itself – Achan. His fault was sin. Joshua's fault was lack of wisdom and of dependence.

Joshua was, at his level for that day, cautious. The reconnaissance party he sent out reported the facts – "they are but few", and a judgment, "let not all the people go up". And so, out of the hundreds of thousands available and eventually required, Joshua, at their word, sent about three thousand men, "and they fled before the men of Ai" (verse 4). What was worse, there were casualties.

VERSES 6-9

At last Joshua and the elders are on their faces before Jehovah to enquire of Him. Their despair is recorded in verses 7-9. The parabolic nature of the history requires a vivid realisation of their predicament. Israel was completely surrounded by an alien and hostile population. They were entirely shut up to only two alternatives – victory or annihilation. There was no help and retreat was impossible.

There is a most important lesson here arising from the application of all this to the Christian's warfare in heavenly places. The stark dilemma which faced Israel scarcely exists for him. In the case of Israel, deliverance from Egypt, the experience of Jehovah's provision during the forty years in the wilderness, and the fight for Canaan, were gone through separately. There was no choice at this stage, no possibility of avoiding conflict in Canaan by going back to the wilderness. All this is because the loving wisdom of our God has given to the Christian the records of these phases of Israel's experiences standing in the Word. They stand there *not for Israel*, but for the Christian so that we may, for our guidance in the path of life, study each as a separate existence. But, in what corresponds to them in the Christian's experience, they represent things that should go on side by side simultaneously. And here is the crux of the matter. It is possible for the Christian to settle down and enjoy the world; it is, in a sense open to the Christian to be satisfied with the experiences of God in the pilgrimage, and so avoid the conflicts of Canaan. Let us make no mistake, the Christian experiences which correspond to "the manna and the springing well", and the pillar of cloud and fire, are very, very wonderful. But to opt for the wilderness and thus draw back from Canaan is to forfeit communion with God in "the things that He hath prepared for them that love Him" – things so rare and precious that eye hath not seen them, nor ear heard, neither have they entered into the heart of man – things centred on Christ in glory, and to know the love which passeth knowledge. It is possible for the Christian, unlike Israel, to choose, or to slip carelessly into this option, and very many Christians do so. Do you?

At this point let us search our hearts. Am I avoiding the conflict of Ephesians chapter six altogether by setting my sights on easier things? Or by the disobedience which permits the Christian to love the world? Are we making full use of the wisdom of God in giving us these things in separate tableaux so as to help us to be clear-cut in our commitment to realising deliverance from Egypt, divine supplies for the wilderness, *and* also victory and rest in the land of promise?

VERSES 10-15

I think it was Spurgeon who entitled a sermon on verse 10 "Unseasonable Prayer". It was indeed so; "Get thee up; wherefore liest thou upon thy face?" It was not a time for prayer, but for action. Israel had sinned. Jehovah's reply seems to indicate that Joshua ought to have known the true state of affairs, by enquiring of Jehovah before the assault on Ai. So the truth would have emerged before the defeat and loss. The action required was to detect and root out the accursed thing. In the language of Ephesians 4:27 they had, "given place to the devil". Sinful behaviour on our part can and will, in our spiritual warfare, give place for the devil.

VERSES 16-21

A substantial part of the sections we are now considering (verses 13-18), deals with the searching process by which the accursed thing was revealed. By this we are led to a more pressing attention to the "searching" of Psalm 139:1, 23-24. This attitude of David must not be thought of as spiritually morbid or diseased. It existed alongside the most intense joy of God. Perhaps we should say rather that such joy in God as David displays – and we covet – could only exist alongside the willingness, nay, the desire, to be searched by God. So, as we read these verses, their lesson will not be lost if David's prayer is put frequently upon our lips, and in our hearts; "Search me, O God, and know me: try me, and know my thoughts: and see if there be any wicked way in me, and lead me in the way everlasting".

We now come to the heart of this part in the history in Achan's confession. Joshua's fault lay in not enquiring of Jehovah, and the discipline was *defeat*. Achan's fault was in the accursed thing, and the punishment was *death*. Achan represents something in the Christian, and not a Christian in person. There is that in me which responds to the attractions of the detestable evils of Ephesians 5:5. It is this man who must be brought under death, the death of Christ.

In our narrative, the first step into disaster was "I saw" (verse 21). Here is a glimpse of the moment when Achan

THE VALLEY OF ACHOR

discovered that the accursed thing can assume an immensely attractive and seductive appeal, while being unmistakeably Canaanite and coming under the ban. The sultry gleam of the gold and silver and the brilliant colours of the garment of Shinar overcame Achan's separation to Jehovah's ban, led him to desire, and finally to action – "I took".

What is detestable in the eyes of Jehovah and fatal to His worship, can be 'goodly' (attractive) in the eyes of the flesh. Among the things that Achan 'saw' was 'a goodly garment of Shinar'. This latter was the name of the country in which Babylon was to develop, and to become a fatal snare to Israel. The 'goodly' aspect of what came out of Mesopotamia is vividly portrayed in the prophets (read Jeremiah 10:9 and Ezekiel 23:5-6). We have already spoken about that which is put to death in ourselves. Here we learn of its attractive aspect in the eyes of the flesh.

Achan's actions and thoughts he gives in strict detail. "I saw – I coveted – I took". The last step is worthy of note – "I hid". In several of those feelings which would make up for the Christian "the accursed thing", there is something distinctly inward, hidden in the heart, nursed and meditated there, so that they are not allowed to appear on the surface. Two such evils are covetousness (Ephesians 5:3) and malice (Ephesians 4:31). The suggestion of feeding mentally on such things is clear in 1 Peter 2:1, as also the need to deal with them conclusively.

VERSES 24-26

There follows a solemn account of events in the valley of Achor. The name of this location occurs in other Scriptures – notably Hosea 2:15. It appears that the names of both Achan and Achor refer to the *trouble* which came on Israel because of Achan's sin. It is wonderful to read in Hosea "I will give her ... the valley of Achor for a door of hope". These words are to enable Israel to see beyond the 'trouble' spoken of by Hosea, to the final blessing, when she shall be restored. If we ask, concerning this sad chapter, what light and stimulus does it provide for us, it is that self-judgment must have a just and sensitive place in our lives. This is surely a lesson supremely applicable and worthwhile for the days in which we live. The assurance is given so long afterwards by Hosea that the process of self-judgment portrayed in the valley of Achor is the sure door of hope for the future. And this is true to our narrative, for from this moment there were no more military defeats, no more battle casualties, but unbroken victory.

CHAPTER 8

VERSES 1-29

These verses are occupied with the victorious assault on Ai. The critical point is poignantly described in verse 20 "And when the men of Ai looked behind them, they saw, and behold, the smoke of the city ascended to heaven, and they had no power to flee this way or that way".

Here the word of Jehovah entered into the realm of explicit tactics, as was so often the case with David long afterwards, and it was obeyed. There was assurance and promise, but then the explicit clarity required, "lay thee an ambush". Many alternatives would present themselves: to repeat the tactics of Jericho? a frontal assault again? a patient siege? a parley? an ambush? It is difficult to avoid the belief that if we were willing to listen, and above all, committed to simple obedience, the Lord would give certain communication of His mind as to action in the Christian warfare: prayer, ministry, visits, forgiving some

THE VALLEY OF ACHOR

individual brother or sister, using some detail of the armour.

Since the final plan was simply obedience to Jehovah's command, it succeeded; and through the stern trial of the valley of Achor, the only defeat Israel suffered in the field was changed to victory. Thus we have seen in Jericho the principles underlying victory, and in Ai the great warning of the principles of defeat, and at the same time the way the valley of Achor is the door of hope. These are immense lessons for the Christian's warfare in heavenly places.

9. Mount Ebal and Mount Gerizim

READ JOSHUA 8:30-35

In a letter to the editor of Scripture Truth *accompanying this chapter, the author spoke of the shortage of written ministry on the chapters in Joshua ahead. So this and the following chapters are particularly the outcome of direct consideration of the verses alone. He also spoke of much help for himself gained from these meditations. While help received from others is valuable, there is special profit in close and first-hand living with the Word alone.*

We are first introduced to these two locations in Deuteronomy 11:26 to 30, part of the long discourse delivered by Moses "in the plains of Moab by Jordan near Jericho". "Behold, I set before you this day a *blessing* and a *curse*; a blessing if ye obey the commandments of Jehovah your God ... and a curse, if ye will not obey. ... And it shall come to pass, when Jehovah thy God hath brought thee in unto the land whither thou goest to possess it, that thou shalt put the blessing upon mount Gerizim, and the curse upon mount Ebal." The translation of verse 30 seems to present difficulty, and it seems to me most meaningful in J.N.Darby's *New Translation*: "Are they not on the other side of Jordan, beside the oaks of Moreh (Shechem), beyond the way toward the going down of the sun (the west) which crosses the land of the Canaanites". The words seem to draw attention to the hazardous nature of this journey of thirty miles across unconquered territory to perform a very public ceremony taking possession of Canaan in the name of Jehovah with burnt offerings and peace offerings. Nothing could more distinctly proclaim the presence of Jehovah with his people to fulfil His promises with a mighty hand.

Deuteronomy 27:2-26 also deals with the events on these mountains. There is considerable difference of detail between Deuteronomy 27 and our text in Joshua 8, but we do not concern ourselves with these, but study the passage in Joshua as it lies before us. At the same time the emphasis in verses 34 and 35 on the scope of the reading permits us to take account of the blessings and the curses in Deuteronomy 27:14 to 30:20. The latter extends to the captivity, the dispersion and the restoration of Israel still in the future.

The future of Israel in literal fulfilment of the promises made to Abraham was mentioned in chapter one of these studies. In the intervening chapters our thoughts have been entirely on the typical meaning of this book. We have seen it as a book of history which is also a book of pictures illustrating in detail the Christian's warfare in heavenly places as set forth in the Epistle to the Ephesians.

In meditating on this portion of the book of Joshua we are constrained to return to emphasise most strongly that the promises made to Abraham and Israel remain to be fulfilled to the last letter. It is important, therefore, to see precisely the close connection between these blessings and the promises.

Read carefully Deuteronomy 28:3-6. These blessings apply to a people who belong to this earth. They apply to the literal Israel in the literal Canaan and to no one else. They belong "in the land which Jehovah thy God giveth thee" and nowhere else (verse 8). The sphere of their application is clear: "thy body ... thy ground ... thy cattle ... thy sheep" (verse 4); "thy basket ... thy store" (verse 5).

The outworking of the blessings and the curses is continued into the far distant future in the conversion and restoration of Israel after the captivity and dispersion. Are the blessings promised by the prophets of Israel to apply after this interval of millenniums still the same in character? Indeed they are. Read of Israel's final conversion in Deuteronomy 30:6, and in verse 9 the nature of the blessings thereafter to be restored to them: "the LORD thy God will make thee plenteous in every work of thy hand, in the fruit of thy body, and in the fruit of thy cattle, and in the fruit of thy land, for good". Read also Jeremiah 31:12. The last words of this blessing reveal the absolute finality of this blessing for Israel, and that blessing is still appropriate to a people belonging to earth and not to heaven. "Therefore they shall come and sing in the height of Zion, and shall flow together to the goodness of the LORD, for wheat, and for wine, and for oil, and for the young of the flock and of the herd: and their soul shall be as a watered garden: and they shall not sorrow any more at all."

At this point we return to our principal theme, the instruction given in this book in a *typical* way regarding the Christian's Canaan.

It is once again to Ephesians that we turn to find the nature of the blessings bestowed upon us in Christianity. "Blessed be the God and Father of our Lord Jesus Christ, who has blessed us with all spiritual blessings in heavenly places in Christ." Is Jehovah now the name of God in (this) action? No; an immense advance has been made. The same God, but now using a Name unknown to Israel: the Father (see Ephesians chapters 1 to 3). May we never forget or fail to adore the divine love that has given the Christian knowledge of that new Name. The summit of the divine love for man is in it. The place where these heavenly blessings dwell – is it Canaan? No; the Christian's Canaan is 'heavenly places'. This expression, while not synonymous with heaven, nevertheless clearly centres on heaven, for this is where Christ appears in glory. Are these blessings of the city and the field, of cattle and sheep, of basket and store? No; they are blessings in the spiritual realm. Do they stem from Abraham? They are 'in Christ', and stem from Abraham only in the sense that Christ is Abraham's seed.

The great value of having these earthly blessings brought before us would be to stimulate the spiritual exercise of meditating in detail on the blessings set out primarily in Ephesians chapters 1 to 3. We have no light in ourselves to realise such blessing, and the apostle's prayer underlines this. He prays (1:18) for the enlightening of the eyes of our hearts, so that we may possess and enjoy them, have their grip over us increased, and be deepened in our response to God.

Let us notice just two parallels. Deuteronomy 28:9a seems to be matched by Ephesians 1:{3-}4b.

"The *God and Father* of our Lord Jesus ... *has chosen us* in Him before the foundation of the world, that we should be holy and without blame *before Him* in love."

"Jehovah shall establish (*hath chosen*, {Deuteronomy} 7:6) thee an holy people *unto Himself.*"

Jehovah the God of Israel, while saying "ye shall be holy, for I am holy", had so far revealed Himself as One whose holiness requires obedience of the "touch not, taste not, handle not" kind. How different the connections when this word is quoted in the New Testament: (1 Peter 1:16) – "not fashioning yourselves according to the former lusts" {1 Peter 1:14}. The holiness of "touch not the unclean thing" is directly contrasted with "perfecting holiness" in "cleansing ourselves from all filthiness of the flesh and of the spirit" in 2 Corinthians 6:17 and 7:1. The special point to note, however, in the first of the spiritual blessings in heavenly places in Ephesians 1:4 is that holiness here is not that of state but of standing. Under the eye of God the believer is now given a standing in Christ according to which he possesses that moral character of blameless holiness and love in which alone God can delight, because it is His own moral perfection of God fully revealed. That this holiness should now be the believer's state as well as his standing is one of the chief burdens of the later part of the epistle. All this broaches themes of surpassing splendour. God has reached out to achieve His own joy in putting upon the believer all that perfect delight in His Beloved One by blessing them in Christ. Here is the centre of God's counsel and purpose of blessing "before the foundation of the world".

The second parallel relates to Deuteronomy 28:12. "Jehovah shall open unto thee his good treasure". What a beautiful verse is this! "the heaven to give the rain unto thy land in his season, and to *bless* all the work of thy hand". The blessings on Mount Gerizim all relate to these chapters in Deuteronomy which Joshua proclaimed. In every case when the land is described there is emphasis on the various features setting out Jehovah's "good treasure, the rain". It will be helpful to distinguish two aspects of the blessings of Canaan. First, *the nature of the land*, so explicitly contrasted with the land of Egypt whence Israel had been redeemed. This has already been underlined and will be considered in greater detail. Secondly, there is *Jehovah's good treasure, the rain*, on which we must now meditate further. There can be little doubt as to the meaning for us in Christianity of this feature; it is the gift of the Holy Spirit. At the moment of the pouring out of the Holy Spirit on the little band about to become the Church, Peter quotes the Old Testament promise: "he will cause to come down for you the rain. ... And it shall come to pass in the last days, saith God, I will pour out my Spirit upon all flesh" (Joel 2:23 and 28) What was poured out like rain on the waiting believers in Acts 2 was the Holy Spirit. And this is abundantly amplified regarding the Church (and not at that time the pouring out of the Spirit on all flesh still future), in the express context of the Christian's struggle, in the Epistle to the Ephesians. Let us pray as we read, that God will grant us to realise the distinct greatness of the gift of the Spirit in this Epistle. It is "the wealth of the Father's glory" (3:16) in order "that Christ may dwell in your hearts by faith; that ye, being rooted and grounded in love, may be able to comprehend with all saints what is the breadth, and length, and depth, and height; and to know the love of Christ, which passeth knowledge, that ye might be filled with all the fullness of God."

It is to many a familiar study to trace the theme of the Holy Spirit through the Ephesian epistle. Let us notice afresh its salient features, bearing firmly in mind as we do so its relevance to the fight. The theme begins in 1:13-14 where we find expressions such as 'promise', 'inheritance', and 'possession' very specifically connected with the same expressions in Joshua (for example 'promise' 22:4; 23:5, 10, 15; 'possession' 12:1; 22:4; 'inheritance' 11:23, with 54 more references).

In times when a form of Christianity which has spread like a fire over the world seems to leave the impression that God's purpose in the gift of the Spirit is achieved in the miraculous powers which accompanied it in the early days, it is of supreme importance to devote a major measure of attention to the spiritual exercises emphasised in the Ephesian epistle and, for example, in 2 Corinthians. What, in the daily exercises of your Christian discipleship is meant for you by the words occurring in 2 Corinthians 3:3; "the epistle of Christ written, not with ink, but *with the Spirit of the living God* ... in the fleshy tables of the heart"?

As has just been remarked, Jehovah's good treasure, the "rain unto the land" (our present meditation), corresponds to the pouring out of the Spirit at Pentecost, never to be repeated or withdrawn. The individual believer comes into the blessing of this original outpouring 'on believing' the word of truth, the gospel of salvation. At the moment of such saving faith the believer receives the Spirit, and the indwelling Spirit is the seal and the earnest of the future inheritance. In the present life the believer possesses no part of the inheritance. He possesses the EARNEST, and the word clearly means that the Spirit's indwelling is our present enjoyment, and the certainty of our future possession of that inheritance. What is the inheritance? Do not think lightly of the question or the answer. All "the exceeding riches of His grace" and "the exceeding greatness of God's power" are in it. It is nothing less than a universe where every trace of evil is done away, and which is penetrated in its remotest detail with the beauty and the glory of the Father's Beloved One.

It would not be fitting, in writing on the book of Joshua, to enter on a detailed exposition of Ephesians, but let us admit that our great lack in these matters is exercise in private and in detail with the Lord and His Word. Jeremiah's word is especially applicable here: "Thy words were found, and I did eat them; and they (became) the joy and rejoicing of my heart". Let us go away from this page and apply ourselves in Jeremiah's way of exercise to *the words* of Ephesians regarding the experiences which accord with the believer's reception of the Holy Spirit; "Access by one Spirit to the Father" (2:18), "Strengthened with might … in the inner man" (3:16), "There is one body and one Spirit" (4:4), "Grieve not the Holy Spirit of God" (4:30), "Be filled with the Spirit" (5:18), "Take … the sword of the Spirit which is the Word of God" (6:17), "Praying always with all prayer and supplication in the Spirit" (6:18). These *words* just quoted lead us on from the basic fact of the gift of the Spirit (that is, His outpouring corresponding to Canaan's blessing, "the rain from heaven"), to the way in which the Spirit's power flows out in the details of life (corresponding to the springs and wells of Canaan, our next theme).

In coming to an end of our consideration of the blessings on Mount Gerizim we must not overlook the danger of despising the blessing. Many in Israel, back to Esau, despised the blessing. "Yea, they despised the pleasant land, they believed not his word" (Psalm 106:24). Two references have already been made to 1 Corinthians 2:7 to

3:3. It will be of great value to read this passage again, and to pause to meditate earnestly upon it. First, there is a most beautiful statement of the Christian's Canaan. "Eye hath not seen, nor ear heard, neither have entered into the heart of man, the things which God hath prepared for them that love him." Next, *rain from heaven*, the work, once for all, of the Holy Spirit; "But God hath revealed them to us by his Spirit, for the Spirit searcheth all things, yea, the deep things of God".

Can it be that the reader feels that he is satisfied not to face the toil and prayer of spiritual exercise? If such be the case, then the apostle's conclusion is extremely searching: "the things of the Spirit of God ... are spiritually discerned ... and I, brethren, could not speak unto you as unto spiritual, but as unto carnal, even as unto babes in Christ. I have fed you with milk, and not with meat; for ... ye are yet carnal: for whereas there is envying, and strife, and divisions, are ye not carnal ... ?" When the Christian is in this manner assailed by the works of the flesh, he is to remember the victory of Joshua's first command, against the Amalekites. Moses puts his finger on the sore in Deuteronomy 25:18. It was "the hindmost ... all that were feeble behind thee", in fact the stragglers, hanging back in the race to enter Canaan, who fell victims to Amalek, the flesh.

Returning to 1 Corinthians 2, the conclusion of the matter is that the apostles (Paul in particular), received the Holy Spirit's revelation of this mystery and of these precious things. By the same Spirit they themselves understood them; and lastly, by the same Spirit they were given the words of God to communicate them to us. The living Holy Spirit uses the priceless treasure of Holy Scripture to lead us into all the truth.

So far in this chapter we have considered the blessings on Mount Gerizim. We must have a few words on the curse on Mount Ebal. In the charge given by Moses as recorded in Deuteronomy 27, the curses only are to be declaimed on Mount Ebal. They set out in detail the abominable practices from the beginning associated with the name Canaan. The blessings *and* curses set out in the later chapters are quite different in character. The curses in chapter 27 specify the evil behaviour; the blessings and curses in the later chapters give the adverse results of disobedience and the favourable results of obedience.

Just as we turn to the Ephesian Epistle for instruction on the blessings in Christianity, so Galatians deals with the curse; and we rejoice to learn there that there is no curse in Christianity: "Christ hath redeemed us from the law, being made a curse for us: for it is written, cursed is everyone that hangeth on a tree" (3:13). It is with this last passage that the curses to be declaimed from Mount Ebal end: "Cursed is every one that continueth not in all things which are written in the book of the law to do them" (Galatians 3:10).

The book of God ends with the blessing flowing with the "pure river of water of life ... out of the throne of God and of the Lamb ... and there shall be no more curse" (Revelation 22:1-3).

10. The Land and Nations of Canaan

READ JOSHUA 9:1-2

Arising from these particular verses, a survey is made of 'the land', and the inhabitants of the land of Canaan. In looking at the physical features of that land, and of the foes that resisted the possession of the land, the spiritual meaning for believers today is important to gather. These matters are highlighted here.

We now enter upon the account of the main campaigns, beginning with the first verse of chapter 9 and culminating in the words "and the land had rest from war" – the last words of chapter 11. Chapter 12 is occupied with summaries of Israel's victories, so that the section on which we now enter extends from 9:1 to 12:24. It is divided into four sub-sections: these are the episode of the "wily" action of the Hivites of Gibeon, 9:3-27; the campaign in the south, 10:1-43; the campaign in the north, 11:1-22; and the list of kings smitten, 12:1-24. Thus Israel possessed, as described in chapters 10 and 11, the central bulk of Canaan, the two main campaigns dealing with regions which afterwards became the kingdoms of Judah and Israel.

Verse one of chapter nine is evidently of great importance for the understanding of the inspired narrative. Statements of similar pattern occur, in addition to 9:1, in 10:40, 11:2, 11:16 and 12:8. Each of these verses contains a selection, different in each case, of phrases describing the configuration of the land; and three (that is 9:1, 11:2 and 12:8), contain a list of the nations encountered. These latter, the nations, we will consider later; let us first look at the details of *hills and valleys*. Why are they given so prominent a place in Joshua? It is because they are the details of the unique feature of the land of promise: the way in which Jehovah's treasure, "the rain of heaven" becomes available, so that Canaan was a land blest above all lands. The key verse is Deuteronomy 8:7, which we must have in full: "For Jehovah thy God bringeth thee into a good land, a land of brooks of water, of fountains and depths that *spring out of valleys and hills*". At a stroke this verse connects the hills and valleys of Canaan with fountains and wells and springs of water. The rain is "Jehovah's treasure", and is given directly by Him: springs and wells and fountains are open to man's neglect or hostility to destroy them, and to man's diligence to care for and use them.

The idea that hills and valleys (the word is '*shephelah*'), the high and the low immediately beside each other, constitute a land configuration most conducive to the appearance of springs and fountains and brooks, is most elaborately confirmed by the study of the geology of Palestine.

There are two passages of Scripture to which the mind turns for the most precious light on fountains, springs and wells – John 4:6-14 and 7:37-39. "The water that I shall give him shall be in him a well of water springing up into everlasting life". And, "If any man thirst, let him come unto me and drink. He that believeth on me, as the scripture hath said, out of his belly shall flow rivers of living water: – (this He spake of the Spirit, which they that believe on him should receive: for the Holy Ghost was not yet given; because that Jesus was not yet glorified)." Response to these pictures in Joshua, and to the Lord's words we have read, is, in the introductory stage an intensely individual matter. The reiterated 'he', 'him', 'if any man' underlines this. The spiritual exercises are prayer, meditation on Scripture as the Lord's own words to us, and self-judgment. The last-named is perhaps least thought-of, and at the same time the most necessary. The reasons are that unworthy behaviour "gives place to the devil", letting the enemy in; and it grieves the Holy Spirit of God, our only power for victory (Ephesians 4:25 to 5:5).

This is perhaps the place to widen our concept of the Christian's Canaan. Hitherto we have confined our thoughts to the "heavenly places" of the Ephesian epistle. In a sense this is right, but the expression in the original is "heavenly things" or "the heavenlies". In Ephesians the context justifies the insertion of "things" as in the AV {margin (Ephesians 1:3)}. Exactly the same expression occurs once elsewhere, John 3:12: "I tell you of heavenly things". Here the context justifies the additional word "things", but the expression is the same. The "earthly things" of which the Lord speaks are clearly concerning the new birth. The "heavenly things" concern eternal life. This Scripture joins together with John 4:14 just quoted ("a well of water springing up into everlasting life") to lead us to think of this theme of transcendent beauty, eternal life, as within the scope of the Christian's warfare. This receives strong confirmation from 1 Timothy 6:12, "Fight the good fight of faith, lay hold on eternal life".

Needless to say, in such a context we must look to the final great end of all the Son reveals regarding eternal life; "this is life eternal, that they might know thee (the Father) the only true God, and Jesus whom thou hast sent". From any conceivable point of view John's finality of truth in John 17:3 must be put alongside Paul's finality of truth in the Mystery, "that ye might be filled with all the fullness of God".

Some of the most memorable and cheering passages of Scripture regarding the land of Canaan deal with its springs and fountains and wells. We end these thoughts with some of these. What a power they possess to stir the heart!

"With joy shall ye draw water out of the wells of salvation" (Isaiah 12:3). "A garden inclosed is my sister, my spouse; a spring shut up, a fountain sealed ... a fountain of gardens, a well of living waters, and streams from Lebanon" (Song of Solomon 4:12, 15). "My people {...} have forsaken me, the fountain of living waters ... what hast thou to do in the way of Egypt, to drink the water of Sihor? or what hast thou to do in the way of Assyria, to drink the waters of the river?" (Jeremiah 2:13, 18).

Who can forget David longing for a drink from the water of the well of Bethlehem? or Isaac, digging and redigging the wells of Canaan? This latter episode speaks vividly of the Christian's diligence in finding refreshment in the Word, so amply rewarded; and also of the need for battle, because the enemy is always active to stop the wells with earth. Isaac's story also reminds us that every generation has to re-dig the wells for itself, a most challenging truth for each individual reader.

We have made use of 9:1 to explain the great importance of understanding why these repeated details giving the configuration of the land are so prominent. As this verse stands, however, its function is to provide an introduction to the whole war. It is a description of the entire land of Canaan from the mountains of Lebanon in the north, to the wilderness in the south. Between the Mediterranean and Jordan, three longitudinal belts are to be distinguished. Alongside the Jordan runs a line of mountains comprising the hill countries of both Samaria and Judah. Westward of these, runs a belt of lowlands named in ancient and modern times the Shephelah. Westward again is the coastal plain. These three correspond to the words in 9:1, "hills", "valleys" (the Shephelah), and "all the coasts of the great sea" up to Lebanon. This verse does not distinguish the north from the south (the Negev), and is thus a background to the whole war.

We come now to the list of the nations of Canaan in the latter part of verse 1. Obviously its prime interest for the Christian reader of Joshua is that they represent our enemies in the conflict of Ephesians 6. In verse 11 of that chapter we meet the principal foe – the devil. But there is an hierarchy of hostile evil revealed in verse 12. Our struggle is not against flesh and blood – a fairly definite allusion to the war in Joshua. Our struggle is in the spiritual realm, heavenly places. The total list of other beings existing and acting at this level are: God, the devil, angels, demons, and man. Man, and man only, is open to the influence of beings at all three levels. And so there is ranged against the Christian, and active whether he is active or not, this hierarchy of purely spiritual powers.

Perhaps they can use appeals at the level of the soul ("I see the sights that dazzle, the tempting sounds I hear"), but act directly on the Christian's spirit.

Here is the list:– the devil/principalities/powers/the rulers of the darkness of this world/spiritual wickedness in heavenly places.

Probably we ought to bring in "the spirit that now worketh in the children of disobedience" ({Ephesians} 2:2), and we certainly ought to take account of light cast by the book of Daniel on the existence and activity of spiritual powers relative to Israel in a hostile way. Especially to be noted is the conflict in the spiritual arena to be seen in Daniel 10:13 and 20. Michael is "the great prince which standeth for the children" of Judah (12:1). Gabriel is the one sent to help Daniel (9:21). And he says "the prince of the kingdom of Persia withstood me" (10:13). These are spiritual conflicts concerned with the earthly Israel and Judah. All this is the scripture background to the Christian's warfare with evil powers arrayed against him and aiming to prevent him "standing", and "having done all to stand" in possession and enjoyment of the spiritual blessings in heavenly places in Christ – which are the substance of the Epistle to the Ephesians.

It must be important that we receive some help from the book of Joshua on this theme. The three elements Joshua presents as forming the hostile power are (1) the kings, (2) the city states, and (3) the nations. (1) and (3) are found here in 9:1, and all three appear, for example in 10:5. As the narrative develops we shall observe these distinctions, but at the moment we must concentrate on the nations; it is with them that the abominable religious practices are found.

145

Seven nations are named by Moses in Deuteronomy 7:1, "greater and mightier" than Israel, but to be "cast out" before them. These same seven names occur once in Joshua 24:11 – where it is stated that they were all met at Jericho. Apart from the last reference, only six nations are named in Joshua; the missing name is Girgashite.

It seems clear that the meanings of the names is connected with nothing more than the kind of country in which they lived. High lexicographical authority (Gesenius-Davies) has given them as follows: Hittite – 'sons of terror'; Amorite – 'highlander'; Perizzite – 'countryman'; Hivite – 'villager'; Jebusite – 'trodden down', perhaps implying 'city dweller'; and Canaanite – 'lowlander'. The order of names in the lists varies bewilderingly, but is perhaps a reflection of varying importance in the localities due to frequent migrations.

The original authority for the nations of Canaan is, of course, Genesis 10, and Genesis 11:2 indicates we have to think of constant migrations. Chapter 10:15-19 deals with the way in which this part of the earth was peopled by the descendants of Noah after the flood (verse 32). It is not easy to distinguish names of individuals from those of countries. For example, Sidon in verse 15 is the name of Canaan's firstborn, but in verse 19 has become the name of a location. Canaan, with whom verse 15 begins, was, according to 9:18 the grandson of Noah, but his place in verse 15 seems to indicate that he took rank as a son of Noah. The mysterious curse of Genesis 9:25 rests on Canaan personally of all the family of Noah, and this casts light on the divine edict for the extermination of the Canaanites in Joshua. If we compare Genesis 9:22 and 23 with Leviticus 18:3, 7, and 27 we see the close connection between Canaan's offence and the edict of destruction against the Canaanites. These scriptures, taken together with the curses declaimed on Mount Ebal, show clearly that the main area of such mortal offences against God was that of perversions in Canaanite religious practices of God's ordinances relative to men and women and marriage.

There are two points for special notice. The inclusive name for all the peoples named in verses 15 to 18 is Canaanite, and in the same verse *migration* in a north-easterly direction is indicated. Note also that the migration results in the Canaanite occupying the exact territory afterwards throughout Scripture called "the land of Canaan". Tracing these names through the story of Abraham, we arrive at the following summary:

(a) The whole of the land of Canaan was called in Scripture sometimes the land of the Canaanites and sometimes the land of the Amorites. These were especially the nations named for destruction.

(b) But within the land of Canaan the Canaanites specifically occupied certain areas of the lowlands. These were the coastal strip as far north as Aphek (Joshua 13:4), and the lowlands about Jordan (Arabah). Joshua 11:3 thus refers to "the Canaanite on the east and on the west".

(c) Also within the land of Canaan, the Amorites' territory was the hill country of Judah. I cannot find any indication that the hill country of Ephraim was reckoned Amorite. In transjordan, the two important kingdoms overthrown were specifically Amorite; Sihon in Heshbon, and Og king of Bashan. These lands were both high mountains.

(d) Certain nations are joined with the Amorites as mountain peoples in Joshua 11:3; "and the Amorite, and the Hittite, and the Perizzite, and the Jebusite in the mountains".

(e) In the verse just quoted the Hivites seem to be separated from the other peoples mentioned. The narrative in chapter 9 shows the Hivites acting extremely independently.

For the present we cannot specify in more detail the distinguishing features of these nations, but as we proceed through the following chapters, we must keep these names in mind, in order to note what special features of hostile power are portrayed in them. In the case of the encounter immediately following in chapter 9 there can be no doubt: the Hivite episode highlights the peril in "the wiles of the devil".

11. The Wiles of The Gibeonites

READ JOSHUA 9:3-27

In our comment on the defeat at Ai, and especially on the lessons there learned by Israel, the words occur: "from this moment there were no more military defeats, no more battle casualties, but unbroken victory". This, in exact terms was true, and of immense import. Nevertheless we have before us in chapter 9 the story of the defeat of a different kind which contains lessons for the Christian's warfare.

The background is the general mobilisation of all the nations of Canaan to "fight with Joshua and with Israel". But a section of one nation, the Hivites, resorted to a different approach – "they did work wilily". Joshua admits this description of their approach: "wherefore have ye beguiled us?" In our quest to find the significance, if possible, of each of the nations so frequently listed in this book, here is the first answer: the Hivites represent the *wiles* of Satan (Ephesians 6:11), and the *beguiling* of the serpent (2 Corinthians 11:3).

On a superficial reading of this episode, we might be tempted to regard it as a kind of false start – an insignificant preliminary. Not so! It was the only action in the whole campaign which produced definite gain to the Canaanites and clear loss of territory for Israel. And its importance for us is underlined by the fact that the only battle act specifically named at first in Ephesians 6 is "the wiles of the devil"! Let us never take lightly the danger presented to us by the *wiles* of the devil.

It will be helpful at this point, to have before us the full passage referred to in 2 Corinthians 11:2-3: and very moving it is. "For I am jealous over you with a godly jealousy: for I have espoused you to one husband, that I may present you as a chaste virgin to Christ. But I fear, lest by any means, as the serpent *beguiled* Eve through his subtlety, so your minds should be corrupted from the simplicity that is in Christ". Remembering that the main text of our warfare – the Ephesian epistle – is the epistle of the Church as the Bride of Christ, how poignant is this appeal for singlehearted fidelity to Christ in the waiting period. The actions of the devil, given in the AV in 2 Corinthians happen to be, for our assistance, alliterative. Against our first coming to faith, *blinding* (4:4). Against our faithful continuance, *beguiling* (11:3). And the enemy still has in his armoury, *buffeting* (12:7).

Let us now pray most earnestly that the Lord may grant us a really helpful reflection on the enemy's wiles, as illustrated in this chapter, so that we may find light on dealing with the wiles of the devil. We must seek answers to questions as follows: 1. What were the aims of the deceit? 2. What were the means employed? 3. What countermeasures are suggested?

First we must dispel any idea, which some commentators have suggested, that the Israelites were at fault in seeing in these strangers valuable allies in the coming hostilities. Nothing could look less warlike, nor less likely to be effective allies than the stream of bedraggled humanity which was seen entering the camp of Israel that day. The fault of the people and their leaders lay elsewhere, as we shall see. These newcomers were not representing themselves as fighting allies, but as suppliants.

THE AIMS OF THE DECEIT

The extent of the knowledge possessed by the Hivites is clear in verses 9, 10 and 24; they came "because of the name of Jehovah thy God; for we have heard the fame of Him, and all that He did in Egypt, and all that He did to the two kings of the Amorites". They knew that the coming of the Israelites meant extermination for all the Canaanite nations. Only by representing themselves as not Canaanites at all, but nationals of some land outside the confines of Canaan, could they escape death under the ban.

The application of this to ourselves and our warfare is deeply significant and solemn. The aim of the wiles of the devil is, in large part at least, to cause the Christian to slip, easily and painlessly, into the assumption that behaviour which in fact would rob him of the precious things of his Canaan is outside the ban, and not therefore to be put to death. At this point I ask the reader to turn back to Chapter 8 and re-read the sections "In the church epistles" to "thy members should perish" on page 122, and also "Achan represents something in the Christian" on page 126 to "portrayed in the prophets" on page 127. In this connection, note particularly the word 'covetousness'.

THE MEANS EMPLOYED

They disguised themselves, using the most meticulous care to change every detail of their appearance and baggage, so as to look like people who had travelled for weeks or months. By the spoken word they presented themselves as a delegation of harmless and foreign origin.

The effect of the Word of God on the believer is to make sin appear as "exceeding sinful". On the contrary the means whereby Satan achieved his end was to make the sin of eating of the forbidden tree look good, pleasant and desirable, and to deny its evil consequences. It is all one with his changing himself into an angel of light. If our consciences were awakened to this danger, it would not be long before we would observe exactly this thing taking place in our own hearts.

COUNTERMEASURES

The one great error stated here in the Word to have been the cause of the downfall (verse 14), was that the people, the princes and Joshua "asked not counsel at the mouth of the Lord". And the one great safeguard for the believer today is just this, to ask for counsel at the mouth of the Lord. For us, of course, the basis of such a safeguard is constant, regular, and diligent application to the written Word of God. For them, it was complete in that it contained all they needed to enjoy and possess Canaan. For us it means that in the most final sense the Scriptures we hold in our hands contain "all the truth" – the *ne plus ultra* of God's revelation ("nothing beyond").

First, application to this Word needs to be done for a continuous, day by day bringing of each mind and heart into its light, so that it may be in all circumstances "a lamp unto my feet and a light to my path" (Psalm 119:105). To work at this constantly, with our conscience alert, is no heavy burden, as the psalmist shows clearly. But in effect it means to be wearing the "whole armour of God" every day – and thus to be enabled to stand against the wiles of the devil, and to quench all the fiery darts of the wicked one (see Ephesians 6 again).

In addition, of course, there is the full privilege of coming at any time to the throne of grace, to find mercy and grace to help in time of need. For us, such uses of the Scriptures make available to us "counsel from the mouth of the Lord".

What of the future of these Hivites in Israel? There is a slight ambiguity occasioned by the reference in 2 Samuel 21:2. It is there stated by the author of the passage that "the Gibeonites were not of the children of Israel, but of the remnant of the Amorites". This, however, could refer not to the existing state of the Gibeonites, but, taking the statement simply, to their origin. They might be compared on this point with the case of Rahab, who was fully taken in to be reckoned an Israelite. Other references to these people tell that these four cities became part of the tribe of Benjamin, and that they were amongst the exiles returned from Babylon, still as part of the tribe of Benjamin. In verses 23 and 27 we learn that they became permanently hewers of wood and drawers of water "for the altar of the Lord", surely a privileged position. Hewers of wood and drawers of water were among the "strangers within thy gates" (Deuteronomy 29:1-15). This latter is a class frequently mentioned in the Old Testament, and as such could have access to all the privileges of Israelites. It thus appears probable that these Hivite cities were rendered, by the wiles of the Gibeonites, permanently unavailable to Israel to possess and enjoy. It was a defeat for Israel unequalled at any other time.

Finally, let us note verse 17. "Now their cities were Gibeon, and Chephirah, and Beeroth, and Kirjath-jearim". Happily, these names are among the easier names to interpret: in order, they mean, hill, village, wells, and city of trees. If reference is made to the description, at the beginning of the previous chapter, of the physical features of Canaan which make it blest above all lands, it will be recognised immediately that these four place names describe a corner of Canaan in which its delights were concentrated. The names describe an area of peaceful habitation in a shaded, well-watered, and fertile location. In other words, the cities lost to Israel by the grave failure to keep in mind the word of the Lord, were among the choicest in the land. How urgent for us are the spiritual lessons drawn out in this chapter.

It is now more than time we had some direct meditation on the substance of the 'spiritual blessings in heavenly places' (Ephesians 1:3) which are the Christian's Canaan. It will be worthwhile to attempt to include some such thoughts, at this moment on 1 Corinthians 2:9, but in later chapters too.

In 1 Corinthians 1:17 to 2:6 so much is said in deprecation of wisdom, that an observer might be imagined to comment: "is your message then foolishness?" To seize the emphasis in context, we might, perfectly permissibly, insert the emphatic 'do' in 2:7 so as to read: "we *do* speak wisdom", but a new and different wisdom, wisdom of God, hidden wisdom, ordained of God before the world. In verse 9 we have the only statement of the content of this wisdom, the mystery, that *this* epistle affords:

"Eye hath not seen, nor ear heard, neither have entered into the heart of man, the things which God hath prepared for them that love Him."

The negatives of this verse (not, nor, neither) seem to have two implications. The first is that man's means of knowing, the channels open to him by which ordinary knowledge reaches him, are all incapable of reaching this mystery. It must remain inaccessible to man, since he possesses no other channel for knowledge. "But God" begins the next verse. God has intervened "for them that love Him". "But God hath revealed them unto us by His Spirit; for the Spirit searcheth all things, yea, *the deep things of God*". Here are the wells (Beeroth) of the Christian's Canaan. "The Spirit ... shall be in him a well of water springing up into everlasting life" (John 4:14).

The second implication of the negatives is that the quality of the knowledge of this mystery is superlative; it exceeds infinitely, in beauty and in satisfying power, all that the mind and heart of man is capable of encompassing.

At this point it seems desirable to bring forward for repetition a quotation from the {previous} chapter: "The spiritual exercises are prayer, meditation on the Scriptures as the Lord's words to us, and self-judgment". And so, at this moment it is our prayer that the Lord Himself may be heard saying to each, "Eat, O friends; drink, yea drink abundantly, O beloved" (Song of Solomon 5:1).

12. The Day When the Sun Stood Still

READ JOSHUA 10

Plainly with this chapter we reach a high point in the book of Joshua, and, as the author indicates, the highest point of exaltation and triumph now occupied by Christ in glory can be seen indicated there. It is something absolutely central to the proper appreciation of Christian truth and its outworking in our lives.

We need to sense the amount of careful study our author has devoted to this book. These are not at all well-trodden areas, judging by the paucity of thorough coverage of them by earlier respected authors. I have felt the value of his treatment of this chapter with particular force.

We now enter upon the two great battle chapters of our Book. In its place – Joshua 3:7 – we noted a remarkable word from Jehovah to Joshua: "This day will I begin to magnify thee in the sight of all Israel". I think we shall see that the chapters now before us record the completion of this process. In the day when Jehovah delivered up the Amorites before Israel, and the sun stood still at the

156

command of a man, then the Word records: "there was no day like that before it or after it" {10:14}. When the confederate hosts under Jabin of Hazor were utterly destroyed at the waters of Merom, then it is recorded "As the LORD commanded ... so did Joshua; he left nothing undone of all that the LORD commanded Moses" {11:15}. And at the end of the chapter, "And the land had rest from war" {11:23, RV}. Joshua was magnified, honour put on him in the eyes of the people, and, as it must be, in the eyes of their enemies.

We have been tracing parallels between the books of Joshua and Ephesians, and it is obviously of first interest to enquire if there is such a parallel at this point. The counterpart of the magnifying of Joshua is very plainly to be seen in that epistle: it is the work and triumph and exaltation of Christ. The exposition of these tremendous truths is centred on Ephesians 1:19-23 and 4:8-10. At this point it will be helpful to bring forward the consideration from our chapter of verses 28-43. Here we have a practically word-for-word repetition of these few verses describing Joshua's destruction of the five Amorite cities. In each of the five cases the phrase is repeated: "Joshua and all Israel with him". It seems evident in this phrase attention is drawn to those cases, the bulk of the book of Joshua chapters 1-12, in which Joshua fights the battles and gains the victories *with* and *for* all Israel, clearly distinguishing them from other cases in which battle, victory and possession are the result of individual faith and initiative. In the latter class are the achievements of Caleb and Othniel (Joshua 15:13-19) and other instances in the early chapters of the book of Judges. This distinction is paralleled by way of type in Ephesians by the distinction between the victory of Christ, now in glory

157

(1:9-23 and 4:8-10), and the fight of the saints against principalities and powers in 6:11-19.

In greater detail let us attempt to seize the parallels between "all Israel *with* him", in Joshua 10, and "quickened ... and raised *with* Christ" in Colossians 2:12-13. The parallel is more complete in Ephesians: "quickened together *with* Christ" (2:5), "raised *together* in Christ" and also "made to sit *together* in heavenly places in Christ" (2:6). These results of the victory of Christ are secure for eternity. We are contrasting them with the warfare of the saints, found in Ephesians 6:12, whereas, alas, only partial and so often temporary victory is obtained. These thoughts will, we most earnestly pray, prompt us to concentrate heart and mind to muse on these chapters of conflict and victory, and to see in them power to move us deeply concerning the battles which raged over the cross and the grave of the Lord Jesus – battles which have resulted in His victory and present exaltation at God's right hand in glory. The unique blessing with which believers of the church dispensation are privileged is that they are united to Christ where He is in heavenly glory by the Holy Ghost sent down from that place. The direct relevance of this to our theme of victory over the nations of Canaan (representing principalities and power in heavenly places) is explicit in Colossians 2:15; "having spoiled principalities and powers, He made a show of them openly, triumphing over them in it".

Before a few comments in order on our chapter, a preliminary word may show how the annihilation of the forces of Jabin of Hazor fits in with what has been suggested above. This was the greatest assemblage of kings and nations and their hosts: but it was "of the LORD ... that He should destroy them utterly" {11:20} so that "the land had rest from war". We are intended to see how complete and final this was. It depicts and confirms the completeness which we must see in Ephesians, regarding the heavenly glory of Christ at the right hand of God. In both cases the victor immediately dispenses the fruits of victory. "When He ascended up on high, He led captivity captive, and gave gifts unto men" (Ephesians 4:8). It is a remarkable fact that this expression "led captivity captive", quoted here from Psalm 68, first appears in Scripture in Judges 5:12 regarding a later Jabin, king of Hazor, and his destruction. I feel at liberty to take account of this fact in considering Joshua 11:17 as a pointer to Ephesians 4:8.

VERSES 1-5

We meet here a special section of the nations of Canaan – "*the five kings of the Amorites*" (verses 5 *et al*). The form of the phrase seems to suggest that they were in some way the totality of the Amorites, at least in this area. It compares with the similar expression "the two kings of the Amorites", in Heshbon and Bashan. Wherever examples are required of luxuriant vegetation, then Bashan and Gilead are sure to be mentioned. Taking account of the cities listed in verse 5, it is clear that these Amorite kings possessed some of the choicest cities of the land, which, earlier and later, were the cherished dwelling-places of Israel. Who can forget the description of Jerusalem, the first of the cities named here, in Psalm 48? "Beautiful for situation, the joy of the whole earth, is mount Zion". Hebron, already an Amorite city, was the chosen dwelling-place of Abraham and Isaac.

Thus we see that the cities or locations fought for in contest with these Amorite kings became the dwelling-places in which the wealth and beauty of Israel's inheritance is prominently displayed.

159

The attack of this confederacy of Amorite kings was not immediately directed against Israel. Evidently they thought to discourage any further adhesion of Canaanites to Israel by destroying Gibeon, a great royal city. Israel was drawn into this conflict by their treaty with Gibeon, but it was of the LORD that Israel should meet and destroy the Amorites, and Joshua took it as from Him.

VERSES 6-11

In these verses we meet again the unchanging importance of Gilgal in this war, and consequently are reminded of the need for the Christian to return again and again to *self-judgment*. If we neglect this, we shall be weak, and the flesh will betray us. It appears that the distance to and from Gilgal was sometimes very great, but nothing must prevent Israel's return thither after *every* episode. We must repeat the meaning for us of the return to Gilgal. It is exactly Colossians 3:5, 8. Several references have been made in these pages of the critical importance of self-judgment in the life of the Christian. The writer must not be ashamed of this repetition, and it is earnestly desired that the reader, rather than permitting a rejecting response, be moved to a firm purpose to seek help in every reading of Scripture to promote it.

The repetition of the word 'camp' {verse 6} here is significant. The phrase is "and Joshua returned, and all Israel with him, unto the camp to Gilgal" {verse 15}. There is no word in this book describing a permanent residence, a house. Israel was still on full war footing: and war demands discipline. And this is very true of the Christian warfare. Verse 9 expresses the very spirit of discipline, something very close to self-judgment, and the LORD gave the victory. He cast great stones upon the enemy, and soon after responded with the immensely greater event at Ajalon.

VERSES 12-14

We cannot be surprised when the Spirit of God speaks thus: "there was no day like that before or after it". It was preceded by a vigorous night-march of some twenty miles; the fighting must have begun at dawn; as the fleeing Amorites tumbled down the pass from Beth-horon towards shelter in their fenced cities, Jehovah's artillery slew more than Israel's swords. But now "the sun was westering. It wanted but an hour or two, and its sudden disappearance would bring on the {rapid} eastern twilight, whilst the moon's pale face appearing over the purple waters of the great sea was waiting to lead on the night"[12], which would rob Israel of the completion of their victory. It was a moment for the great spirit of Joshua, doubtless moved on by the Spirit of the LORD, to call for an intervention which would convert that already memorable victory into an event unique in all time. "The sun stood still".

In verse 12 two addresses are attributed to Joshua. "Then spake Joshua to the LORD", and he said, "Sun, stand thou still". To this command, the sun rendered immediate obedience, thus displaying the fact that, in response to the prayer, the LORD had exalted Joshua above the rulers of the day and night. In praying thus, Joshua is a lesson to the believer in all ages; when the believer prays that God will open the eyes of his heart, he is asking for an event just as much outside the realm of nature as the sun standing still. Nevertheless we believe that in this

[12] F B Meyer (1847-1929), *Joshua and the Land of Promise*, London: Morgan & Scott, 1893.

command Joshua is, in the typical way, standing beside the Lord Jesus Himself in His exaltation.

It is time we turned specially to a passage to which these events directly lead us, Ephesians 1:19-23. This passage is the concluding section of the apostle's first prayer in that epistle. We shall never enter upon the possession of the Christian's Canaan unless we make and carry out a firm purpose to use this prayer in definite spiritual exercises of prayer, meditation and self-judgment. Verse 18 presents an opportunity for the kind of "arrow" prayer on the pattern of Nehemiah in the presence of Artaxerxes (Nehemiah 2:4) addressed to the God of our Lord Jesus Christ: "O God, open the eyes of my heart ...". It is here we meet for the first time the Christian's enemies in the characteristically Christian warfare, "principalities and powers", only to learn immediately that Christ is "far above" them. And this position of Christ is the very heart of Christianity. If we have been permitted to seize this truth, then there is cause for thanksgiving, for it is not generally recognised in Christendom. Any reference to "Jesus" can with practical certainty be referred to the Jesus of the Gospel story. But the saints' union with Christ where He is now seated (at God's right hand in heavenly places), a union in His body which is the church (effected by the descent of the Holy Ghost from that place above), is the unique privilege of believers in this present period, and in no other. This centrally important though much-ignored truth will bear being repeated. I believe we have a pointer to it in the exaltation of Joshua above the sun in victory over the Amorites.

VERSES 15-39

These verses indicate the prosecution of the victory to the utter destruction decreed by Jehovah. "Joshua left none

162

remaining, but utterly destroyed all that breathed, as the LORD God of Israel commanded" {verse 40}. Verses 22-27 record the execution by hanging of the five Amorite kings, and it is noteworthy that Joshua is careful to obey, not only the special commands for this time, but also the written word in Deuteronomy 21:23: "His body shall not remain all night upon the tree, but thou shalt in any wise bury him that day ... that thy land be not defiled, which the LORD thy God giveth thee for an inheritance". Verses 28-39 came forward for special comment, when attention was drawn to the importance of the phrase "Joshua and all Israel with him".

VERSES 40-43

It is important to see the great part played in this day's work in the totality of Joshua's conquest of Canaan. In these verses we have the geographical summary specifying exactly the region conquered in the narrative of chapter 10. It should be compared with the summary in 9:1, concerning which we stated, in its place, that "it is a description of the entire land of Canaan, from the mountains of Lebanon in the north, to the wilderness in the south", indicating how widespread was the alarm created among the kings and nations of Canaan. Here in these verses we learn that the first actual campaign was confined to the southern portion of the land. The kind of country included brings in the well-known words – the hill country, the Negev, the Shephelah, and the Springs. The place names in verse 41 clearly delineate the whole of Canaan south of Gibeon, that is, Judah, eventually to become the southern kingdom. All the names of places smitten in chapter 10 are in fact listed in the inheritance of Judah in chapter 15. There is no reference here to the nations encountered.

163

13. "And the Land Had Rest From War"

READ JOSHUA 11

The chapter studied here completes the record of the overthrow of the powers resisting the occupation of the land by Joshua and Israel. With chapter 12 (which lists kings subjugated in this action) it rounds off the first section of the book. Thereafter the division of the land, and its allocation to the various tribes, is recounted.

The name of Charlotte Elliott is well known as the authoress of perhaps the best known and loved of all gospel hymns: "Just as I am, without one plea". What appears to be much less known is her hymn of foes and battle, of armour and ambush, which begins, "Christian, seek not yet repose"[13]. This hymn was adapted to the book of Joshua {by Mrs Hazel Dixon}: and {her additional} verse 3 in particular relates to our theme in chapter eleven. Taking account of the fact that Merom was the mustering point for un-numbered foes, Charlotte Elliott's verse {4} is so exactly applicable as to qualify to be the heading to this chapter:

---

[13] No. 282, *Psalms and Hymns and Spiritual Songs: Selected 1978*, Wooler: Central Bible Hammond Trust, 1978

164

"Principalities and powers,
Mustering their unseen array,
Wait for thy unguarded hours:
Watch and pray".

VERSES 1-5

The usual geographical summary in verses 2 and 3 is not for the purpose of specifying the area of conquest, but to underline the immense zeal of Jaban king of Hazor in sending out king's messengers to summon all the nations of northern Canaan to repel the invader. This is one of several instances when all the seven nations are listed, with the exception of the Girgashites. These were the kings of the area which afterwards under Jeroboam became the kingdom of Israel. This enormous host, "as the sand which is upon the sea shore in multitude, with horses and chariots very many" {verse 4}, joining its several units together, mustered at the "waters of Merom", perhaps ten miles north-west from Hazor, and encamped there "to fight against Israel".

VERSES 6-14

It would appear that Jabin looked on the waters of Merom as so strong a position that his forces were halted there and awaited the attack of the Israelite army. Once again Jehovah intervened with His word to Joshua; it must always be an element of sovereign importance to have the Word of the Lord injected into any situation. We see Joshua in all this narrative as primarily presenting to us the activity of the Lord Jesus Himself in gaining the victory. But this is by no means an obstacle to our taking to ourselves the lessons of these means to victory, especially where it stresses the commanding need for our receiving the Word of God for every situation. What came from Jehovah to Joshua, probably while still at Gilgal, was a word of encouragement, of promise, and assurance: "be not afraid, tomorrow about this time, I will deliver them up"; and it also was a word of command for the destruction of that mighty force in its totality.

We would do well to pause at this point to take account of the richness of provision for the needs of God's people in all ages to give them victory in His Name. There is in these words to Joshua what meets the needs of men and women with respect to the emotions, the intellect, and the will. It is no small part of our spiritual exercises to note and apply such communications as they appear in every reading of Scripture. No doubt stimulated by such communications Joshua once again acts with such vigour as to achieve a surprise attack "by the waters of Merom ... and Jehovah delivered them into the hand of Israel, who smote them, and chased them" in three scattering directions, until they left none remaining. And Joshua ended the distant pursuits with exact obedience to Jehovah's command: "he houghed[14] their horses, and burnt their chariots with fire".

At this point Joshua turned his attention to the great city Hazor, formerly the "head of all those kingdoms" and its king, Jabin. "Utter destruction" had been the command given to Moses by Jehovah (Deuteronomy 20:17) and passed on to Joshua. The head of all those heathen kingdoms could not have any part in the new dominion of Jehovah; and utter destruction and burning with fire was the fate of Hazor, that great city.

There has been some confusion about the meaning of verse 13. On a point such as this, that is, of pure language and grammar, NEB must be treated with respect. "The cities whose {ruined} mounds are still standing (presumably when the book of Joshua was written) were

---

[14] {Hamstrung}

not burned by the Israelites; it was Hazor alone that Joshua burned". This has the air of a matter remitted to the archaeologists. Of all the cities involved in this part of the narrative, none has yet been excavated except Hazor, and the excavation of the Hazor tell[15] showed unmistakably that Hazor did suffer an utterly destructive burning at this time. The confirmation of the fate of the other cities still lies under the soil of Palestine.

We may note words spoken regarding a later Jabin, king of a later Hazor: "Arise, and take thy captivity captive"; and these words take us to Ephesians 4:8 (where they are quoted from Psalm 68:18) to which our studies in this part of Joshua lead us – to the position of Christ which He now occupies as a consequence of His victory by death and resurrection over principalities and powers. It is there we now behold Him by faith, seated at the right hand of His Father and awaiting the moment when His foes will be made His footstool. In the meantime this view of Joshua leads us to see that it is from this position, consequent upon His victory over spiritual foes, He distributes the fruits of His victory (Ephesians 4:7-11). There is a clear parallel between this distribution in Ephesians 4 and the allocation of the inheritance in Canaan which occupies so large a part in the later chapters of Joshua from chapter 14.

Ministry which arises from such a study as that of the book of Joshua, and indeed all true ministry, must have for a major objective the stimulation of the spiritual exercises which have been mentioned several times. As we think of the passages in the Epistle to the Ephesians so recently considered, the writer and the reader might well be moved to question their own hearts. How much time have I spent in the contemplation of Christ in glory? This

---

[15] {A hill formed over the remains of successive ancient settlements}

is certainly the theme for meditation which lies before us – and what a deeply moving theme it is!

In this epistle the person of Christ comes before us from beginning to end in His heavenly resurrection glory "far above all heavens" and seated at God's right hand. Very early (1:6), as the Father's Beloved, He is the measure of the believer's acceptance, and the thought of the Father's pleasure in Him is a never-failing source of delight throughout Scripture. Meditation on Christ in His suffering and death of course takes primacy, because of the Lord Jesus's institution of His Supper – but let us never forget the central place in Christianity of the upward look to Him where He is.

Moreover, in addition to these general remarks on the importance of meditation, there are exceeding great and precious promises explicitly attached to contemplation of Christ in glory. The theme of 2 Corinthians 3 is "the glory that excelleth" shining now in the face of Jesus glorified. The metaphor is exceedingly striking. No terrestrial object takes on a new image more rapidly than a mirror turned to face a new object. The change is instantaneous. In the metaphor, the open face of the believer is the mirror, and the fullness of the blessing for the believer is unmistakable; "we all, with open face beholding as in a glass the glory of the Lord, are changed into the same image from glory to glory, even as by the Spirit of the Lord" (verse 16). The action of the believer to receive such a blessing, is to "turn to the Lord" in the way of meditation.

The words "and the land had rest from war" (11:23), already referred to, are followed in chapter 12 by the list of kings east of Jordan destroyed by Moses and Israel, as well as the list of kings smitten by Joshua and Israel on the west side. Thus chapter 12 completes the account forming the first main division of the book of Joshua. We shall not comment in detail on chapter 12, since it is a summary of what has gone before. What lies before us next therefore is the account of the allocation of the tribal inheritances, beginning with chapter 13.

Here the author's work ends: the conquest completed, Canaan possessed.

Appendix: The Sound of The Silver Trumpets

READ NUMBERS 10:1-10

These few verses are full of practical instruction to us if we look at them carefully. At the end of chapter 9 we find the tabernacle reared up and the principle established that the people's journeyings or encampments were governed entirely by the movement of the cloud. Between the last verse of chapter 9 and verse 11 of chapter 10 (when they make their first journey from Sinai to Paran) we read the instructions for the manufacture and use of the two silver trumpets. For this reason we believe that the silver trumpets speak of God's direction and ordering of the movements of his people.

Let us notice that they were to be made of one piece, reminding us that God speaks with one voice at all times, to all peoples, in all circumstances. His revelation of Himself and of His purposes has developed but never contradicted anything previously revealed. The message of both Old and New Testament hangs together in one: God's answer to the question of sin for His glory through the redemption that is in Christ Jesus. The comparison of a few verses from the Old and New Testaments serves to illustrate this:

"Without the shedding of blood is no remission" (Hebrews 9:22; compare Leviticus 17:11).

"The just shall live by faith" (Habakkuk 2:4; Romans 1:17; Galatians 3:11; Hebrews 10:38).

"Be ye holy, for I am holy" (Leviticus 11:44; 1 Peter 1:16).

"The Gospel of God which He had promised before by his prophets in the Holy Scriptures" (Romans 1:2).

Let us now consider the use of the trumpets. Every movement of the children of Israel was to be in accord with their sound. We can state that the trumpets governed (1) their *worship*, (2) their *walk*, (3) their *warfare*, (4) their *welfare*.

So it should be with us. Our whole Christian life, individual or collective is not left to our own ideas; it is not left to tradition, to convenience, or to novelty, but must be regulated always and only by the sound of the trumpet, that is, by the testimony from God Himself in His Word.

WORSHIP

(We take the word *worship* in its widest sense.) The trumpets were used to call the assembly together. In the New Testament there are at least four calls to come together.

Firstly, *to remember the Lord.* Acts 20:7 — "upon the first day of the week when the disciples were come together to break bread". Their objective was to remember the Lord. It was not even to listen to the ministry of Paul (though he was present and did speak to them at length later); they came together with the primary thought of remembering the Lord. In the passage in 1 Corinthians 11, speaking of the Lord's supper, the phrase *come together* occurs five times. Have we obeyed the sweet notes of the silver trumpets calling us to "do this in remembrance of me"?

Secondly, the call to "come together" is for *edification*. In 1 Corinthians 14 the emphasis is on that which is profitable for the edifying of the church, as Paul exhorts (verse 12), "that ye may excel to the edifying of the church". Two verses in this chapter bring a special appeal to us along the line we are considering:

(i) "If therefore the *whole* church be come together into one place" (verse 23). Whenever there is a meeting of the assembly for worship, prayer, edification, etc., it is the responsibility of each of us if at all possible to be there. "The whole church into *one* place." While there certainly is a place for special activities for young people, for women, or other particular groups, let us be careful to bear in mind that the real objective for the assembly is for all to be gathered together in one place. This is the pathway to a united, healthy assembly life. Gospel outreach work, Sunday School, young people's groups, camps, etc., depend on entirely different considerations, and nothing said is intended to discourage such valuable work; where however it is a question of those in the church, the *whole church in one place* is the norm. In Numbers 10 a blast on one trumpet called the elders. Two trumpets called everybody. There were no other calls for particular groups.

(ii) 1 Corinthians 14:26 reads, "How is it then brethren? when ye come together, every one of you hath a psalm, hath a doctrine, hath a tongue, hath a revelation, hath an interpretation ...". Paul has to appeal for order and decency to regulate this over-enthusiasm. Sadly, one wonders whether the opposite injunction might not be more often required nowadays: "How is it, when ye come together, *not one of you* hath ...."! Let everyone be ready to use the gift that God has given us to edify one another. It is a sad reflection on our spiritual state if, when we come into the Lord's presence we have nothing to contribute.

Thirdly, the call to "come together" is for *prayer*. "And when they had prayed, the place was shaken where they were assembled together; and they were all filled with the Holy Ghost" (Acts 4:31). How desperately we need to know the power of prayer that can shake the place and fill us with Holy Spirit power! The only way to know it is to set ourselves to give Him the absolute authority and priority in our lives, individually and collectively.

Fourthly, there is a call to come together in relation to the *gospel*. Peter went in with Cornelius "and found many that were come together" (Acts 10:27). What a gospel opportunity! Do we not long for occasions like that? They were an expectant company, just ready and open to hear the word: "Now therefore are we all here present before God to hear all things that are commanded thee of God" (verse 33). Why does it not happen like that nowadays? It did not "just happen" then either! Go back to verse 24. Cornelius had "called together his kinsmen and near friends", and because of his previous life and testimony amongst them (see verse 2) they had come. Cornelius had "blown the trumpet".

WALK

The second main use of the trumpets was to order the marching — the walk — of God's people. I would like to illustrate this in the life of the apostle Paul. Please read 2 Corinthians 1:12-22, where we have Paul *listening* for the trumpet, and 2 Corinthians 2:14-16, where we find Paul *sounding* the trumpet.

Paul's listening springs from his rule of conduct, as spelled out in 1:12. "In simplicity and godly sincerity ... we have had our conversation [or, behaved ourselves] in the world." Or, as he says elsewhere, "For me to live is Christ". Paul lived for one purpose alone, and that was to glorify Christ and do His will whatever the cost.

Like all of us, Paul had to make plans for his future movements. He had intended to pay the Corinthians another visit, but had been forced to alter his plans, and some were accusing him of fickleness. In 1:15 we read, "And in this confidence I was minded to come unto you before ... Did I use lightness?" That is, do I say one thing and do another? Paul was listening for the trumpet and, as it did not sound, he did not move. This was more important to him than the criticisms of men. However much he may be misunderstood, however puzzling the pathway may appear, Paul had a glorious resting place where all was absolutely secure. "All the promises of God in him [the Son of God, Jesus Christ] are yea, and in him Amen, unto the glory of God by us" (verses 19-20).

In 2 Corinthians 2:14 (AV margin) we read of "God, who always leadeth us in triumph". Paul is still listening. You can only lead those who are willing to follow. "My sheep hear my voice, and I know them, and they follow me" (John 10:27). But in these verses we also get Paul's *sounding* the trumpet, under a different metaphor. His testimony was, to God, a sweet savour of Christ. It was like the sweet notes of the silver trumpets blown over the burnt offering (Numbers 10:10).

To the perishing Paul sounded an alarm, a smell of death unto death (verse 16), warning them of the consequences of rejecting Christ and continuing in their sins. To the saved he sounded the silvery notes of redemption, life unto life, reminding them of the wondrous realm of blessing into which they had been brought through the redemption that is in Christ Jesus.

WARFARE

Let us notice that it is "war on your land" (Numbers 10:9) to which the trumpets summoned. This reminds us of the exhortation in Ephesians 6:10*ff*, to put on "the whole armour of God that ye may be able to stand ...". It is interesting to notice that in these verses in Ephesians the whole description of the enemy is contained between the two exhortations to "put on the whole armour of God". That armour is sufficient to meet every onslaught. God has "blessed us with all spiritual blessings in heavenly places in Christ", and brought us into the "land of pure delights". The enemy tries to rob us of the enjoyment of this, to prevent us from possessing our possessions. In the physical sense the Israelites would put on the armour, but they also had to blow an alarm with the trumpets. "And ye shall be remembered before the Lord your God, and ye shall be saved from your enemies" (Numbers 10:9). Let us not forget to blow the trumpet. Ephesians 6:18, "Praying always with all prayer and supplication in the Spirit, and watching thereunto with all perseverance and supplication for all saints".

In the heavenlies see that land,
Satan would thine entrance stay;
Thou against his wiles must stand:
Watch and pray.[16]

WELFARE

"Also in the day of your gladness, and in your solemn days, and in the beginnings of your months, ye shall blow with the trumpet, over your burnt offerings ..." (Numbers 10:10). We might say that their crises and their calendar were under the sound of the trumpet. This brings us to the very practical consideration as to where we find our joy and cause of rejoicing. Where do we turn in trouble or distress? How do we regulate our diary? We cannot do more than quote a few verses from James to illustrate these features. Of the "day of your gladness", he says, "Is any merry? Let him sing psalms" (James 5:13). "Rejoice in the Lord alway" (Philippians 4:4). Of the "solemn days", James says, "Is any afflicted? Let him pray". "Comfort ye one another with these words" (1 Thessalonians 4:18). Of "the beginnings of your months", he says, "Ye ought to say, If the Lord will, we shall live and do this, or that" (James 4:15). So it should be with us. Our whole life in every detail should be governed by the testimony of God in His Word, brought home to us in the power of the Spirit until

THE TRUMPET SOUNDS

"In a moment, in the twinkling of an eye, at the last trump: for the trumpet shall sound, and the dead shall be raised incorruptible, and we shall be changed" (1 Corinthians 15:52).

"For the Lord himself shall descend from heaven with a shout, with the voice of an archangel, and with the trump

---

[16] Mrs H Dixon (1923-2015)

of God: and the dead in Christ shall rise first: Then we which are alive and remain shall be caught up together with them in the clouds, to meet the Lord in the air: and so shall we ever be with the Lord" (1 Thessalonians 4:16-17).

No more warfare, no more marching in the wilderness, no more solemn days, for all will be days of gladness — "for ever with the Lord". The last great assembling shout — not just the priests blowing the trumpets, but God, the Lord Himself calling the final glorious "Come together". And for ever *all the church will be together in one place* with the Lord.

Tom Tyson

www.ingramcontent.com/pod-product-compliance
Lightning Source LLC
Chambersburg PA
CBHW071219090426
42736CB00014B/2900